MONEY AND HAPPINESS

Exploring the Intricate Relationship Between Wealth and Well-Being

Dr. Maxwell Shimba

Printed by Shimba Publishing LLC
Printed in the United States of America

TABLE OF CONTENTS

INTRODUCTION

In today's fast-paced world, money is often seen as the key to unlocking happiness. From advertisements promising joy through material possessions to the societal belief that financial success equates to personal fulfillment, we are constantly reminded of the role money plays in our lives. Yet, despite rising incomes and consumer choices, many people find themselves grappling with stress, dissatisfaction, and an elusive sense of happiness. Money and Happiness by Dr. Maxwell Shimba aims to unravel this complex relationship and offer a deeper understanding of how money truly impacts our well-being.

This book takes a comprehensive approach to explore the connection between financial prosperity and happiness. By examining historical perspectives, psychological theories, and contemporary research, it seeks to challenge conventional wisdom and offer fresh insights into the role money plays in our lives. While money is undeniably important in fulfilling basic needs and providing security, Money and Happiness argues that its influence on happiness is far more nuanced. Dr. Shimba will guide readers through key concepts such as the pursuit of material wealth versus life experiences, the impact of financial stress on mental health, and the benefits of generosity and financial mindfulness.

When readers dive into this book, they can expect an exploration of both the scientific and practical aspects of achieving financial well-being. They will gain insights into how different cultures view wealth, how financial management can reduce stress and anxiety, and why balancing personal values with financial goals is critical to lasting happiness. Through case studies, real-life examples, and practical strategies, Money and Happiness provides readers with a roadmap to not only manage their finances better but also lead more fulfilling, purposeful lives. By the end of this journey, readers will have a clearer understanding of how to use money as a tool for happiness rather than a source of pressure or discontent.

DR. MAXWELL SHIMBA

CHAPTER 01

THE QUEST FOR HAPPINESS

The quest for happiness is a fundamental human endeavor, one that has been pursued across cultures and centuries. This universal pursuit has led to countless philosophies, religions, and scientific inquiries all seeking to understand what it means to live a happy and fulfilling life. In modern society, one of the most significant aspects of this quest revolves around the role of money. Can money truly buy happiness? If so, how much is enough? And what are the psychological factors that determine the impact of money on our well-being?

In contemporary discourse, the relationship between money and happiness is a topic of significant interest and debate. On one hand, financial security is undeniably essential for meeting basic needs and providing stability. On the other hand, the relentless pursuit of wealth and material possessions often seems to lead to dissatisfaction and stress rather than true contentment. This book aims to explore the intricate relationship between money and happiness, dissecting the psychological factors that contribute to a fulfilling financial life.

The Importance of Understanding Money and Happiness

Understanding the relationship between money and happiness is more critical now than ever. As the world becomes increasingly materialistic, with consumer culture and economic pressures intensifying, it is essential to examine how these trends impact our mental and emotional well-being. By exploring the nuances of this relationship, we can better navigate our own financial decisions and strive towards a more balanced and fulfilling life.

The desire for happiness drives much of human behavior. Whether through personal achievements, relationships, or financial success, individuals continuously seek ways to enhance their well-being. Money, being a primary means of achieving various goals, naturally becomes a central focus. However, the assumption that more money directly equates to more happiness is an oversimplification. The reality is far more complex, influenced by various factors including psychological predispositions, cultural contexts, and individual life circumstances.

The Dichotomy of Money and Happiness

The dichotomy of money and happiness presents an intriguing paradox. While financial resources are necessary for a comfortable and secure life, an excessive focus on acquiring wealth can lead to adverse effects on happiness. This paradox is well-illustrated by the Easterlin Paradox, which suggests that beyond a certain threshold, increases in income have a diminishing return on happiness. Essentially, once basic needs are met, additional wealth contributes less and less to overall well-being.

At the core of this paradox is the concept of relative wealth. People often measure their financial success not in absolute terms but relative to others. This social comparison can lead to feelings of inadequacy and discontent, even among the wealthy. Moreover, the pursuit of material wealth often comes at the expense of time, relationships, and personal growth—elements that are crucial for a happy and meaningful life.

Psychological Theories on Money and Happiness

To unravel the complexities of money and happiness, it is essential to delve into various psychological theories. These theories provide frameworks for understanding how financial resources influence our emotional and mental states. For instance, Maslow's Hierarchy of Needs highlights the importance of meeting basic physiological and safety needs before one can pursue higher levels of self-actualization and fulfillment.

Another important theory is the concept of hedonic adaptation, which suggests that individuals quickly return to a baseline level of happiness following positive or negative changes in their circumstances. This means that while a significant financial windfall may initially boost happiness, the effect often wears off as people become accustomed to their new level of wealth.

Furthermore, self-determination theory posits that true happiness comes from fulfilling intrinsic needs for autonomy, competence, and relatedness rather than extrinsic rewards such as money. This theory underscores the importance of aligning financial goals with personal values and relationships.

The Role of Culture and Society

Culture and society play a significant role in shaping our perceptions of money and happiness. Different cultures have varying attitudes towards wealth and well-being, influenced by historical, economic, and social factors. For example, individualistic societies may emphasize personal achievement and financial success, while collectivist cultures might prioritize community and relational well-being.

Understanding these cultural differences is crucial for a holistic view of the money-happiness relationship. It also highlights the importance of societal values and norms in shaping individual aspirations and experiences of happiness. In a globalized world, where cultural boundaries are increasingly blurred, examining these diverse perspectives can offer valuable insights into creating a more balanced approach to wealth and well-being.

Objectives of This Book

The primary objective of this book is to provide a comprehensive exploration of the relationship between money and happiness. By examining historical contexts, psychological theories, cultural influences, and practical strategies, we aim to offer a nuanced understanding of how financial resources impact our well-being. This book will:

1. Trace the historical evolution of the concepts of money and happiness, offering insights into how these ideas have developed over time.

2. Define happiness and explore its various dimensions, providing a clear framework for understanding this complex emotion.

3. Examine psychological theories that explain the connection between financial resources and well-being.

4. Discuss the role of basic needs and financial security in achieving happiness.

5. Analyze the impact of wealth on subjective well-being, including factors like income inequality and social comparison.

6. Explore the downsides of materialism and the benefits of prioritizing experiences over possessions.

7. Address the effects of financial stress on mental health and offer strategies for managing it.

8. Highlight the psychological benefits of generosity and altruism.

9. Investigate how money influences relationships and social connections.

10. Consider cultural and societal factors that shape the money-happiness relationship.

11. Provide practical advice on financial management to enhance well-being.

12. Present case studies that offer real-life insights into the money-happiness dynamic.

13. Speculate on future trends in the relationship between money and happiness.

By the end of this book, readers will have a deeper understanding of how to navigate their financial lives in ways that promote true happiness and fulfillment. Our ultimate goal is to empower individuals to make informed decisions that align with their values and lead to a balanced and meaningful life.

CHAPTER 02

THE HISTORICAL CONTEXT OF MONEY AND HAPPINESS

The relationship between money and happiness has evolved over millennia, influenced by cultural, economic, and philosophical developments. By examining historical perspectives, we can gain insights into how different eras have shaped our understanding of this complex interplay. From ancient philosophies to modern economic theories, the nexus between wealth and well-being has been a subject of enduring interest and debate.

Ancient Philosophies and the Pursuit of Happiness

In ancient times, happiness was often seen as a state of being rather than a direct outcome of material wealth. Philosophers like Aristotle and Confucius offered early insights into the nature of happiness and its relationship to external conditions.

Aristotle and Eudaimonia

Aristotle, one of the most influential philosophers of ancient Greece, introduced the concept of eudaimonia, often translated as "flourishing" or "well-being." According to Aristotle, true happiness is achieved through the practice of virtue and the fulfillment of one's potential, rather than the accumulation of wealth. He believed that while material resources are necessary for a comfortable life, they are not sufficient for achieving eudaimonia. Instead, a life of virtue, wisdom, and meaningful relationships is paramount.

Confucianism and Harmony

In ancient China, Confucianism emphasized the importance of harmony, both within oneself and in society. Confucius taught that happiness comes from living a life of moral integrity and fulfilling one's roles and responsibilities within the family and community. Wealth, in this context, was seen as secondary to the cultivation of virtue and the maintenance of social harmony.

Medieval Perspectives: Religion and Asceticism

During the medieval period, religious teachings played a significant role in shaping attitudes towards wealth and happiness. Both Christianity and Islam offered distinct perspectives on the role of money in a fulfilling life.

Christianity and the Virtue of Poverty

In medieval Europe, Christian doctrine often emphasized the virtue of poverty and the dangers of material wealth. Figures like St. Francis of Assisi advocated for a life of simplicity and detachment from worldly possessions. The Bible's teachings, such as the parable of the rich young man and the admonition that "the love of money is the root of all evil" (1 Timothy 6:10), reinforced the idea that spiritual fulfillment and eternal happiness were more important than earthly riches.

Islam and Zakat

In the Islamic world, the concept of zakat, or almsgiving, highlighted the ethical responsibility of the wealthy to support those in need. While Islam does not condemn wealth outright, it stresses the importance of using one's financial resources for the common good and achieving a balance between material success and spiritual well-being. The Quran emphasizes that true happiness comes from a combination of faith, good deeds, and the ethical use of wealth.

The Enlightenment and the Birth of Economic Thought

The Enlightenment era brought a shift in thinking about money and happiness, as new economic theories emerged and the pursuit of personal and societal well-being became intertwined with economic progress.

Adam Smith and the Wealth of Nations

Adam Smith, often regarded as the father of modern economics, introduced the idea that the pursuit of self-interest and economic prosperity could lead to the greater good of society. In "The Wealth of Nations" (1776), Smith argued that individuals seeking to improve their own circumstances would inadvertently contribute to the overall economic development and well-being of society. However, Smith also acknowledged that wealth alone does not guarantee happiness, and he stressed the importance of moral sentiments and social harmony.

Jeremy Bentham and Utilitarianism

Jeremy Bentham, a prominent philosopher of the Enlightenment, developed the theory of utilitarianism, which posits that the greatest happiness of the greatest number should be the guiding principle of ethics and governance. Bentham's ideas influenced economic policies and social reforms aimed at improving the well-being of the population. The utilitarian approach provided a framework for evaluating the impact of wealth distribution and economic policies on overall happiness.

Industrialization and the Modern Era

The Industrial Revolution and the rise of capitalism brought significant changes to the relationship between money and happiness. The rapid economic growth and increased standard of living raised new questions about the sources and sustainability of happiness.

The Rise of Consumer Culture

The 20th century saw the emergence of consumer culture, where material possessions and consumption became central to the notion of happiness. Advertising and mass media promoted the idea that acquiring goods and services was key to achieving a fulfilling life. However, this period also saw growing concerns about the psychological and social costs of materialism, including the erosion of community and environmental degradation.

The Easterlin Paradox

In 1974, economist Richard Easterlin published a groundbreaking study that challenged the assumption that higher income always leads to greater happiness. The Easterlin Paradox revealed that while wealthier individuals within a country tend to be happier than their poorer counterparts, this relationship does not necessarily hold at the national level. Over time, as countries become wealthier, average happiness levels often plateau, suggesting that factors other than income play a crucial role in well-being.

Contemporary Views: Wealth, Inequality, and Well-Being

In recent decades, the study of happiness and its relationship to money has become a multidisciplinary field, incorporating insights from psychology, sociology, and economics. Researchers have sought to understand the nuanced ways in which financial resources influence well-being.

Income Inequality and Social Comparison

Modern research has highlighted the impact of income inequality on happiness. Studies have shown that high levels of income inequality can lead to social tensions, reduced trust, and lower overall well-being. The relative nature of wealth—how one's income compares to that of others—plays a significant role in shaping individual happiness. Social comparison can lead to feelings of inadequacy and envy, even among those who are relatively well-off.

The Role of Financial Security and Stability

Financial security and stability are crucial for mental health and well-being. The ability to meet basic needs, plan for the future, and cope with unexpected expenses significantly influences happiness. Conversely, financial insecurity and debt can cause stress, anxiety, and a diminished sense of control over one's life.

The Happiness of Experiences vs. Possessions

Recent studies have emphasized the importance of spending on experiences rather than material possessions. Experiences, such as travel, social activities, and personal growth opportunities, tend to provide more enduring happiness than the accumulation of goods. This shift in understanding has led to a greater focus on how people allocate their financial resources to maximize well-being.

Tracing the historical context of money and happiness reveals a complex and evolving relationship. From ancient philosophies that prioritized virtue and social harmony to modern economic theories that explore the psychological nuances of wealth, the pursuit of happiness has always been influenced by our understanding of money. By examining these historical perspectives, we gain valuable insights into the enduring questions about how financial resources can enhance or hinder our well-being.

In the following chapters, we will delve deeper into the psychological theories, cultural influences, and practical strategies that shape the money-happiness nexus in contemporary society. By building on the foundation of historical knowledge, we aim to provide a comprehensive guide to navigating the intricate relationship between money and happiness in the modern world.

CHAPTER 03

DEFINING HAPPINESS

Happiness is a universal aspiration, yet it is one of the most elusive and complex concepts to define. Philosophers, psychologists, and scholars have long debated its meaning, resulting in various definitions and theories. To understand how money influences happiness, it is essential first to establish a clear understanding of what happiness entails. This chapter explores the different dimensions of happiness, including psychological well-being, life satisfaction, and emotional fulfillment.

Psychological Well-Being

Psychological well-being refers to the overall mental state of an individual and encompasses various aspects such as emotional balance, personal growth, and positive relationships. According to Carol Ryff's model of psychological well-being, there are six key components:

1. Self-Acceptance: Having a positive attitude towards oneself and accepting multiple aspects of one's personality, including strengths and weaknesses.

2. Personal Growth: The continuous development and realization of one's potential over time.

3. Purpose in Life: Having goals, a sense of direction, and a feeling that life is meaningful.

4. Environmental Mastery: The ability to manage life's demands effectively and create a context suitable for personal needs.

5. Autonomy: The ability to make independent choices and resist social pressures.

6. Positive Relations with Others: Establishing and maintaining quality relationships based on trust, empathy, and affection.

These components collectively contribute to an individual's overall psychological well-being and provide a comprehensive framework for understanding happiness beyond fleeting emotions.

Life Satisfaction

Life satisfaction is another crucial aspect of happiness, referring to an individual's overall evaluation of their life as a whole rather than focusing on specific moments. It involves a cognitive judgment process where people assess their quality of life based on their own criteria.

Several factors influence life satisfaction, including:

1. Material Conditions: Adequate income, stable housing, and access to healthcare are fundamental components.

2. Social Relationships: Strong, supportive relationships with family, friends, and community members.

3. Employment and Work-Life Balance: Meaningful work and a balance between professional and personal life.

4. Physical Health: Overall physical well-being and absence of chronic illnesses.

5. Personal Achievements: Accomplishments in various life domains such as education, career, and personal goals.

Life satisfaction is often measured through surveys where individuals rate their satisfaction with different life aspects on a scale. It provides a broader picture of happiness that encompasses long-term fulfillment and contentment.

Emotional Fulfillment

Emotional fulfillment focuses on the affective aspect of happiness, which includes the presence of positive emotions and the absence of negative emotions. Positive emotions such as joy, love, and contentment contribute to a sense of happiness, while negative emotions like sadness, anger, and anxiety detract from it.

Positive Affect: Experiencing frequent positive emotions such as joy, gratitude, interest, and hope. These emotions enhance well-being and contribute to a more optimistic outlook on life.

Negative Affect: Experiencing infrequent negative emotions such as sadness, fear, and anger. Managing and reducing negative affect is crucial for maintaining emotional balance and overall happiness.

The balance between positive and negative emotions is often referred to as the "affective balance" and is a key indicator of emotional fulfillment. Tools like the Positive and Negative Affect Schedule (PANAS) help measure this balance and provide insights into an individual's emotional state.

Theories of Happiness

Several theories have been developed to explain the nature of happiness and its determinants. Understanding these theories can help us grasp the complexity of happiness and its relationship with money.

Hedonic Theory: This theory suggests that happiness is derived from pleasure and the avoidance of pain. According to the hedonic perspective, the pursuit of enjoyable experiences and the accumulation of positive emotions are central to achieving happiness. This view aligns with the idea that money can buy pleasurable experiences, thereby contributing to happiness.

Eudaimonic Theory: In contrast to the hedonic approach, the eudaimonic theory posits that true happiness comes from living a life of virtue and fulfilling one's potential. It emphasizes personal growth, meaningful relationships, and the pursuit of higher goals. From this perspective, money's role in happiness is secondary to living a life aligned with one's values and purpose.

Self-Determination Theory: This theory highlights the importance of fulfilling three basic psychological needs: autonomy, competence, and relatedness. According to self-determination theory, satisfying these needs is essential for psychological well-being and intrinsic motivation. Financial resources can support these needs by providing opportunities for personal growth, mastery, and social connections.

The Dynamic Nature of Happiness

Happiness is not a static state but a dynamic process influenced by various factors over time. Life events, changes in circumstances, and personal development all impact an individual's happiness. Understanding the temporal nature of happiness is crucial for exploring how money influences it.

Hedonic Adaptation: One of the significant insights into the dynamic nature of happiness is the concept of hedonic adaptation. This refers to the tendency of individuals to return to a baseline level of happiness after experiencing positive or negative changes in their lives. For example, a financial windfall may lead to a temporary increase in happiness, but over time, individuals often revert to their previous happiness levels.

Set Point Theory: This theory suggests that each person has a relatively stable "set point" of happiness that is determined by genetic and personality factors. While life events and circumstances can cause temporary fluctuations, individuals tend to return to their set point over time. Understanding set point theory helps explain why increases in income might not lead to lasting increases in happiness.

Measuring Happiness

Measuring happiness is a challenging task due to its subjective nature. However, several methods and tools have been developed to assess different aspects of happiness.

Self-Report Surveys: These are the most common methods for measuring happiness. Participants are asked to rate their overall happiness, life satisfaction, and emotional experiences. Examples include the Satisfaction with Life Scale (SWLS) and the Subjective Happiness Scale (SHS).

Experience Sampling Method (ESM): This method involves asking participants to report their feelings and experiences in real-time at random intervals throughout the day. ESM provides a more accurate picture of daily fluctuations in happiness.

Behavioral Indicators: Observing behaviors such as social interactions, expressions of gratitude, and engagement in enjoyable activities can provide indirect measures of happiness.

Defining happiness is a complex endeavor that requires consideration of psychological well-being, life satisfaction, and emotional fulfillment. By understanding the different dimensions of happiness and the theories that explain its determinants, we can better examine how money influences it. Happiness is a dynamic process influenced by a variety of factors, including financial resources, but it is also shaped by personal values, relationships, and the ability to find meaning and purpose in life.

CHAPTER 04

PSYCHOLOGICAL THEORIES ON MONEY AND HAPPINESS

Psychologists have long been fascinated by the intricate relationship between money and happiness. Over the years, several key theories have emerged, each offering valuable insights into how financial resources impact our well-being. This chapter delves into some of the most influential psychological theories, including Maslow's Hierarchy of Needs, the Easterlin Paradox, hedonic adaptation, and income satisfaction.

Maslow's Hierarchy of Needs

One of the most well-known frameworks for understanding human motivation and happiness is Abraham Maslow's Hierarchy of Needs. Introduced in 1943, Maslow's theory posits that human needs are arranged in a hierarchical order, with more basic needs at the bottom and higher-level needs at the top. According to Maslow, individuals must satisfy lower-level needs before they can address higher-level aspirations.

1. Physiological Needs: These are the most basic needs necessary for survival, such as food, water, shelter, and clothing. Financial resources are crucial at this level, as they provide the means to meet these fundamental needs.

2. Safety Needs: Once physiological needs are met, individuals seek safety and security. This includes personal safety, financial security, health, and well-being. Money plays a significant role in fulfilling these needs, as it can provide stability, insurance, and a sense of protection.

3. Love and Belongingness Needs: At this level, individuals seek relationships, social connections, and a sense of belonging. While money is less directly related to these needs, it can still facilitate social interactions and opportunities for forming bonds through shared experiences and activities.

4. Esteem Needs: This stage involves the need for self-esteem, recognition, and respect from others. Financial success can contribute to esteem by providing a sense of achievement and status. However, it is essential to note that

true esteem also relies on personal accomplishments and self-worth beyond material wealth.

5. Self-Actualization Needs: At the top of the hierarchy is self-actualization, the realization of one's full potential and the pursuit of personal growth and fulfillment. While financial resources can support self-actualization by providing access to education, hobbies, and travel, the intrinsic motivation to grow and achieve remains paramount.

Maslow's Hierarchy of Needs highlights the role of money in addressing basic and security needs, while also emphasizing that true happiness and fulfillment require addressing higher-level psychological and self-fulfillment needs.

The Easterlin Paradox

The Easterlin Paradox, named after economist Richard Easterlin, presents a critical challenge to the assumption that more money always leads to greater happiness. In his seminal 1974 study, Easterlin found that while wealthier individuals within a country tend to be happier than their poorer counterparts, increases in a nation's average income do not necessarily lead to increases in average happiness.

Easterlin's findings suggest that beyond a certain threshold, additional income has a diminishing return on happiness. This paradox can be explained by several factors:

1. Relative Income: People often evaluate their well-being relative to others rather than in absolute terms. As a result, increases in income may lead to only temporary boosts in happiness if others' incomes rise at the same rate.

2. Social Comparison: Individuals compare themselves to their peers, neighbors, and colleagues. This social comparison can lead to feelings of inadequacy and discontent, even if one's absolute income increases.

3. Hedonic Adaptation: As people become accustomed to higher income levels, their expectations and desires adjust, leading to a return to their baseline level of happiness. This concept is explored further in the next section.

The Easterlin Paradox underscores the importance of considering relative income, social comparison, and adaptation when examining the relationship between money and happiness.

Hedonic Adaptation

Hedonic adaptation, also known as the "hedonic treadmill," is the process by which individuals return to a stable level of happiness despite significant positive or negative changes in their circumstances. This phenomenon explains why the initial joy from a financial windfall or a new purchase often fades over time.

Several factors contribute to hedonic adaptation:

1. Baseline Happiness: Each individual has a baseline level of happiness determined by genetic and personality factors. While life events can cause temporary fluctuations, people tend to revert to their baseline happiness levels.

2. Rising Expectations: As people achieve higher income levels or acquire new possessions, their expectations and desires increase accordingly. This continuous cycle of rising expectations can prevent lasting increases in happiness.

3. Comparative Standards: People compare their current situation to their past experiences and to others' circumstances. These comparisons can lead to dissatisfaction if they perceive themselves as less successful or fortunate.

Research on hedonic adaptation suggests that while money can provide temporary boosts in happiness, its long-term impact is limited. To achieve lasting happiness, individuals should focus on factors that resist adaptation, such as meaningful relationships, personal growth, and purposeful activities.

Income Satisfaction

Income satisfaction refers to the degree to which individuals feel content with their financial situation. It is influenced by both absolute income levels and relative comparisons. Several key factors shape income satisfaction:

1. Absolute Income: Higher absolute income levels can improve financial security and access to goods and services, contributing to greater satisfaction.

2. Relative Income: Individuals often assess their financial situation in relation to others. Income satisfaction can be influenced by social comparisons and perceived fairness.

3. Financial Stability: Stable income and financial security are crucial for income satisfaction. Unpredictable income or financial instability can lead to stress and dissatisfaction.

4. Financial Expectations: People's satisfaction with their income is also shaped by their expectations and goals. Meeting or exceeding financial expectations can enhance satisfaction, while unmet expectations can lead to dissatisfaction.

5. Non-Material Factors: Income satisfaction is not solely determined by material wealth. Factors such as job satisfaction, work-life balance, and overall quality of life also play a significant role.

Understanding income satisfaction provides insights into how people perceive their financial well-being and how money can contribute to or detract from their overall happiness.

Contemporary Research on Money and Happiness

Contemporary research has expanded our understanding of the relationship between money and happiness, incorporating insights from psychology, economics, and sociology. Some key findings include:

1. Experiential Purchases: Spending money on experiences, such as travel, dining, and social activities, tends to provide more lasting happiness than spending on material possessions. Experiences create lasting memories and strengthen social bonds.

2. Prosocial Spending: Using money to help others, whether through charitable donations or gifts, can enhance happiness. Prosocial spending fosters a sense of connection, purpose, and generosity.

3. Financial Health: Financial health, including good money management, low debt levels, and savings, contributes significantly to happiness. Financial stability and the ability to handle unexpected expenses reduce stress and enhance well-being.

4. Work and Income: Job satisfaction and work-life balance are crucial determinants of happiness. Meaningful work, fair compensation, and a healthy balance between professional and personal life contribute to overall well-being.

5. Cultural Differences: Cultural factors influence the relationship between money and happiness. Societal values, norms, and economic conditions shape how people perceive and use money to achieve happiness.

Psychological theories provide valuable frameworks for understanding the complex relationship between money and happiness. Maslow's Hierarchy of Needs highlights the importance of addressing both basic and higher-level needs, while the Easterlin Paradox and hedonic adaptation challenge the notion that more money always leads to greater happiness. Income satisfaction and contemporary research further illuminate the multifaceted ways in which financial resources impact well-being.

By examining these theories and findings, we gain a deeper understanding of how money can contribute to or detract from happiness. The insights from psychological research can guide individuals in making financial decisions that align with their values and enhance their overall well-being.

CHAPTER 05

THE ROLE OF BASIC NEEDS AND FINANCIAL SECURITY

Financial security plays a pivotal role in ensuring that basic needs such as food, shelter, and healthcare are met. These fundamental needs are essential for survival and serve as the foundation upon which higher levels of well-being are built. This chapter will explore how fulfilling these basic needs impacts happiness and examine the threshold at which additional income ceases to significantly enhance well-being.

The Importance of Basic Needs

Basic needs refer to the essential requirements for human survival and functioning. They include:

1. Food and Water: Access to adequate nutrition and clean water is fundamental for maintaining physical health and well-being.

2. Shelter: A safe and stable living environment protects individuals from environmental hazards and provides a sense of security.

3. Healthcare: Access to medical care and health services is crucial for preventing and treating illnesses, ensuring overall physical and mental health.

Meeting these basic needs is the first step toward achieving a stable and satisfying life. Without financial resources to secure these essentials, individuals face significant stress and hardship, which can severely impact their happiness and overall quality of life.

Financial Security and Its Impact on Well-Being

Financial security refers to the state of having sufficient financial resources to meet one's basic needs and handle unexpected expenses. It encompasses having a stable income, savings, and access to credit if needed. Financial security provides several key benefits that contribute to happiness:

1. Reduced Stress: Financial insecurity is a major source of stress and anxiety. Knowing that one's basic needs are met and that there are resources to handle emergencies reduces financial stress and enhances overall well-being.

2. Improved Health: Financial security allows individuals to afford healthcare, nutritious food, and a safe

living environment, all of which are crucial for maintaining physical and mental health.

3. Greater Autonomy: Having financial resources provides individuals with greater control over their lives and the ability to make choices that align with their values and goals. This sense of autonomy is a key component of psychological well-being.

4. Enhanced Relationships: Financial stability can reduce conflicts and tensions related to money within families and relationships, fostering a more harmonious and supportive environment.

The Threshold Effect: When Additional Income Ceases to Enhance Well-Being

While financial security is essential for meeting basic needs, research suggests that beyond a certain threshold, additional income has a diminishing impact on happiness. This phenomenon is often referred to as the "income threshold" or the "diminishing returns of income."

Income Threshold: Studies have shown that once individuals reach a certain level of income that allows them to comfortably meet their basic needs and achieve a reasonable level of financial security, the incremental increase in happiness with additional income becomes smaller. This threshold varies by country and cost of living but generally aligns with middle-class income levels.

Diminishing Returns: The concept of diminishing returns means that each additional dollar of income contributes less to overall happiness than the previous dollar. For example, an increase in income from $20,000 to $40,000 may significantly enhance well-being, but an increase from $100,000 to $120,000 is likely to have a much smaller impact.

Several factors contribute to this diminishing return effect:

1. Hedonic Adaptation: As discussed in the previous chapter, individuals quickly adapt to higher income levels and new material possessions, leading to a return to their baseline happiness over time. This adaptation reduces the long-term impact of additional income on well-being.

2. Relative Comparison: People tend to compare their income and financial status to those of others. As income increases, the reference group often shifts to include wealthier individuals, perpetuating a cycle of comparison and potentially limiting the happiness derived from higher income.

3. Material vs. Non-Material Factors: Beyond a certain point, non-material factors such as relationships, personal growth, and meaningful activities become more significant

determinants of happiness than additional income. Focusing solely on financial gain can neglect these crucial aspects of well-being.

The Role of Financial Security in Different Life Stages

Financial security's impact on happiness can vary across different life stages, reflecting changing priorities and needs.

1. Early Adulthood: In this stage, individuals often focus on establishing their careers, gaining financial independence, and forming stable relationships. Financial security allows for investing in education, starting a family, and building a foundation for future well-being.

2. Midlife: During midlife, financial responsibilities may increase with raising children, purchasing a home, and planning for retirement. Financial security is crucial for managing these responsibilities and reducing the associated stress.

3. Retirement: In retirement, financial security ensures that individuals can maintain their standard of living, access healthcare, and enjoy leisure activities. Adequate savings and pension plans contribute significantly to happiness and peace of mind during this stage.

Strategies for Achieving Financial Security

Achieving financial security involves effective money management, planning, and making informed decisions. Here are some strategies to enhance financial security and well-being:

1. Budgeting and Saving: Creating a budget helps track income and expenses, ensuring that basic needs are met and enabling savings for future needs and emergencies. Prioritizing savings and building an emergency fund are essential steps toward financial security.

2. Managing Debt: Reducing and managing debt is crucial for financial stability. Strategies include paying off high-interest debts first, consolidating loans, and avoiding unnecessary borrowing.

3. Investing Wisely: Making informed investment decisions can help grow wealth and provide financial security in the long term. Diversifying investments and seeking professional advice can mitigate risks.

4. Planning for Retirement: Starting early with retirement savings and contributing regularly to pension plans or retirement accounts ensures financial stability in later life.

5. Financial Education: Increasing financial literacy and understanding money management principles empowers individuals to make better financial decisions and achieve long-term security.

Financial security is fundamental for meeting basic needs and ensuring a stable foundation for happiness and well-being. While additional income beyond a certain threshold may have diminishing returns on happiness, achieving financial security provides significant benefits, including reduced stress, improved health, and greater autonomy. Understanding the role of basic needs and financial security in different life stages and implementing effective strategies for managing money can enhance overall well-being.

CHAPTER 06

WEALTH AND SUBJECT WELL-BEING

Subjective well-being (SWB) is a comprehensive measure of how individuals experience and evaluate their lives. It encompasses emotional responses, domain satisfactions, and global judgments of life satisfaction. Understanding how wealth influences SWB requires analyzing various factors, including income inequality, social comparison, and personal aspirations. This chapter explores these dynamics to provide a nuanced view of the relationship between wealth and subjective well-being.

Defining Subjective Well-Being

Subjective well-being is a multifaceted construct that includes three primary components:

1. Life Satisfaction: This cognitive aspect involves a reflective assessment of one's life as a whole or specific domains, such as work, relationships, and health.

2. Positive Affect: This refers to the presence of positive emotions and moods, such as joy, contentment, and enthusiasm.

3. Negative Affect: This involves the presence of negative emotions and moods, such as sadness, anger, and anxiety.

The balance between positive and negative affect, along with overall life satisfaction, provides a holistic measure of an individual's subjective well-being.

The Influence of Wealth on Subjective Well-Being

Wealth can impact subjective well-being in several ways, both directly and indirectly. While financial resources are crucial for meeting basic needs and providing security, their influence on SWB extends beyond mere material comfort.

1. Direct Effects:

- Basic Needs and Security: As discussed in the previous chapter, wealth ensures that basic needs such as food, shelter, and healthcare are met, which is foundational for well-being.

- Opportunities and Choices: Wealth provides access to a broader range of opportunities, including education, travel, and leisure activities, which can enhance life satisfaction and positive affect.

2. Indirect Effects:

- Social Status: Wealth often confers social status and recognition, which can boost self-esteem and contribute to overall well-being.

- Control and Autonomy: Financial resources offer greater control over one's life circumstances and the ability to make autonomous decisions, both of which are crucial for psychological well-being.

Income Inequality and Subjective Well-Being

Income inequality refers to the uneven distribution of income within a population. It has significant implications for subjective well-being, influencing both individual experiences and societal dynamics.

1. Relative Deprivation: Income inequality can lead to feelings of relative deprivation, where individuals perceive themselves as worse off compared to others. This social comparison can result in dissatisfaction and lower life satisfaction, even among those who are relatively well-off.

2. Social Trust and Cohesion: High levels of income inequality can erode social trust and cohesion, creating a more fragmented and less supportive society. This lack of social capital can negatively impact well-being by increasing stress and reducing a sense of community.

3. Psychological Stress: The stress associated with income inequality can manifest in various ways, including increased anxiety, depression, and health issues. This stress is often exacerbated by societal pressures to conform to certain standards of success and consumption.

Social Comparison and Subjective Well-Being

Social comparison theory suggests that individuals determine their own social and personal worth based on how they compare to others. This process can significantly influence subjective well-being, especially in the context of wealth.

1. Upward Comparison: Comparing oneself to those who are wealthier or more successful can lead to feelings of inadequacy and envy. Upward comparison often results in reduced life satisfaction and negative affect.

2. Downward Comparison: Conversely, comparing oneself to those who are less fortunate can enhance feelings of gratitude and contentment. Downward comparison can temporarily boost subjective well-being, but it may not lead to long-term satisfaction.

3. Impact of Media and Social Networks: Media portrayals and social networks often highlight the lives of the wealthy and successful, amplifying social comparison and its effects on well-being. This constant exposure can skew

perceptions of what constitutes a "good life" and create unrealistic expectations.

Personal Aspirations and Subjective Well-Being

Personal aspirations and goals play a crucial role in shaping subjective well-being. The relationship between wealth and well-being is often mediated by the types of goals individuals pursue and their alignment with personal values.

1. Intrinsic vs. Extrinsic Goals:

- Intrinsic Goals: Goals related to personal growth, relationships, and community involvement are associated with higher levels of well-being. These goals are inherently satisfying and contribute to a sense of purpose and fulfillment.

- Extrinsic Goals: Goals centered around financial success, fame, and social status are often linked to lower well-being. While achieving these goals can provide temporary boosts in happiness, they are less likely to lead to lasting satisfaction.

2. Materialistic Values: Individuals who prioritize materialistic values tend to experience lower subjective well-being. The pursuit of material wealth can lead to a cycle of ever-increasing desires and expectations, which may never be fully satisfied.

3. Goal Attainment and Satisfaction: The extent to which individuals achieve their personal goals also impacts

well-being. Success in reaching meaningful goals enhances life satisfaction, while failure or persistent striving without fulfillment can diminish well-being.

Strategies for Enhancing Subjective Well-Being through Wealth

While wealth alone cannot guarantee happiness, certain strategies can help individuals leverage their financial resources to enhance subjective well-being:

1. Align Spending with Values: Spending money on activities and experiences that align with personal values and interests can enhance life satisfaction and positive affect. This includes investing in relationships, personal growth, and community involvement.

2. Focus on Experiences: Research suggests that spending on experiences, such as travel, hobbies, and social activities, provides more lasting happiness than purchasing material goods. Experiences create enduring memories and strengthen social connections.

3. Practice Gratitude: Cultivating gratitude for what one has, rather than constantly striving for more, can enhance well-being. Keeping a gratitude journal or regularly reflecting on positive aspects of life can foster a sense of contentment.

4. Manage Social Comparisons: Reducing the frequency and intensity of social comparisons can improve

subjective well-being. This can be achieved by limiting exposure to social media, focusing on personal achievements, and surrounding oneself with supportive and non-competitive peers.

5. Set Meaningful Goals: Pursuing goals that are intrinsically rewarding and aligned with personal values can lead to greater fulfillment. Setting realistic and attainable goals, and celebrating progress along the way, can boost well-being.

Wealth has a complex and multifaceted relationship with subjective well-being. While financial resources are essential for meeting basic needs and providing security, their impact on happiness extends beyond material comfort. Factors such as income inequality, social comparison, and personal aspirations play significant roles in shaping how wealth influences well-being.

Understanding these dynamics can help individuals make informed decisions about how to use their financial resources to enhance their subjective well-being. By focusing on intrinsic goals, meaningful experiences, and gratitude, individuals can leverage their wealth to achieve a more fulfilling and satisfying life.

CHAPTER 07

MATERIALISM AND ITS DISCONTENTS

Materialism, the pursuit of material possessions and wealth as a primary source of satisfaction, is often seen as a path to happiness. However, research consistently shows that materialism can lead to decreased well-being and overall dissatisfaction. This chapter explores why materialism can be detrimental to happiness and how shifting focus from possessions to experiences can enhance well-being.

Understanding Materialism

Materialism is characterized by the belief that acquiring and owning material goods is a primary goal and a source of happiness. It involves prioritizing possessions and wealth over other values and aspects of life. Materialism can manifest in various ways, such as the relentless pursuit of luxury items, an excessive focus on consumerism, and equating personal success with financial status.

The Psychological Impact of Materialism

Numerous studies have highlighted the negative psychological impact of materialism on well-being. Some of the key reasons why materialism can be detrimental include:

1. Hedonic Adaptation: Material possessions often provide only temporary boosts in happiness. Once the initial excitement of acquiring a new item wears off, individuals quickly return to their baseline levels of happiness, prompting a cycle of continuous consumption without long-term satisfaction.

2. Unrealistic Expectations: Materialism fosters unrealistic expectations about the role of possessions in achieving happiness. When these expectations are not met, disappointment and dissatisfaction ensue.

3. Reduced Life Satisfaction: Individuals who prioritize material wealth often report lower life satisfaction. The constant desire for more can overshadow other important aspects of life, such as relationships, personal growth, and meaningful experiences.

4. Increased Stress and Anxiety: The pursuit of material wealth can lead to financial stress and anxiety, especially if individuals accumulate debt or feel pressure to

maintain a certain lifestyle. This stress can have adverse effects on mental and physical health.

5. Negative Social Comparisons: Materialism often involves comparing oneself to others in terms of possessions and financial status. These comparisons can lead to feelings of inadequacy, envy, and lower self-esteem.

6. Weakened Relationships: A focus on material wealth can detract from the time and energy spent on building and maintaining relationships. Social connections and meaningful interactions are crucial for well-being, and neglecting them in favor of material pursuits can lead to loneliness and isolation.

The Shift from Possessions to Experiences

Research suggests that shifting focus from acquiring possessions to investing in experiences can significantly enhance happiness and well-being. This shift involves prioritizing activities and interactions that provide lasting memories and personal growth over the accumulation of material goods. Here are some reasons why experiences are more conducive to happiness:

1. Enduring Memories: Experiences create lasting memories that individuals can revisit and cherish over time. These memories contribute to long-term happiness and satisfaction.

2. Enhanced Social Connections: Shared experiences often involve social interactions and connections with others. Whether it's traveling with friends, attending events, or participating in group activities, these interactions strengthen relationships and contribute to overall well-being.

3. Personal Growth and Development: Engaging in new experiences promotes personal growth, learning, and development. Trying new activities, exploring different cultures, and stepping out of one's comfort zone can lead to a greater sense of accomplishment and fulfillment.

4. Reduced Hedonic Adaptation: Unlike material possessions, experiences are less subject to hedonic adaptation. The joy derived from experiences tends to last longer, as individuals continue to reflect on and derive meaning from them.

5. Intrinsic Value: Experiences often align more closely with intrinsic values, such as personal growth, relationships, and meaningful engagement. These values are more strongly associated with long-term happiness than extrinsic values like wealth and status.

Practical Strategies for Shifting Focus

Transitioning from a materialistic mindset to one that values experiences requires intentional effort and reflection. Here are some practical strategies to help make this shift:

1. Reflect on Values: Take time to reflect on your core values and what truly brings you happiness. Identify areas of life that provide intrinsic satisfaction, such as relationships, personal growth, and meaningful activities.

2. Set Experience-Based Goals: Instead of setting goals related to acquiring possessions, focus on goals that involve experiences. This could include traveling to new places, learning a new skill, or participating in community events.

3. Prioritize Relationships: Invest time and energy in building and maintaining relationships. Plan activities with friends and family that create lasting memories and strengthen social bonds.

4. Practice Gratitude: Cultivate a habit of gratitude by regularly reflecting on and appreciating the experiences and relationships that bring joy to your life. Gratitude can help shift focus away from material desires.

5. Limit Exposure to Consumerism: Reduce exposure to advertising and media that promote materialism. Be mindful of how marketing influences your desires and decisions, and seek out content that aligns with your values.

6. Budget for Experiences: Allocate a portion of your budget specifically for experiences rather than material goods.

Plan and save for activities and trips that you will cherish and remember.

7. Embrace Minimalism: Consider adopting a minimalist lifestyle by decluttering and simplifying your possessions. Focus on quality over quantity and invest in items that truly add value to your life.

The Role of Society and Culture

Society and culture play significant roles in shaping attitudes toward materialism and experiences. In many cultures, consumerism is deeply ingrained, and success is often equated with material wealth. To foster a more experience-oriented mindset, societal attitudes and cultural norms need to evolve.

1. Educational Initiatives: Promoting financial literacy and education about the benefits of experiences over possessions can help individuals make informed choices that enhance well-being.

2. Media Influence: Media can play a powerful role in shifting cultural attitudes. Highlighting stories and content that emphasize the value of experiences, relationships, and personal growth can counteract the pervasive materialistic messages.

3. Community Programs: Encouraging community-based programs and activities that promote social

connections and shared experiences can foster a sense of belonging and reduce the emphasis on material wealth.

4. Policy Changes: Policymakers can support initiatives that promote work-life balance, access to recreational activities, and community engagement. Policies that reduce economic inequality and provide financial security can also alleviate the pressures of materialism.

Materialism, with its focus on acquiring possessions and wealth, is often associated with decreased happiness and well-being. The relentless pursuit of material goods can lead to dissatisfaction, stress, and weakened relationships. In contrast, shifting focus from possessions to experiences can enhance happiness by creating lasting memories, strengthening social connections, and promoting personal growth.

By adopting strategies that prioritize experiences over material goods and fostering cultural changes that support this shift, individuals and society can work towards greater well-being and fulfillment. In the following chapters, we will explore additional factors that influence the relationship between money and happiness, including financial stress, the benefits of generosity, and the role of financial management. By building on the insights gained in this chapter, we aim to provide a comprehensive understanding of how to navigate the complex interplay between wealth and well-being.

CHAPTER 08

EXPERIENCES VS POSSESSIONS

The debate between spending money on experiences versus possessions has garnered significant attention in recent years. Research consistently shows that individuals who prioritize experiential spending report greater happiness and life satisfaction than those who focus on acquiring material goods. This chapter investigates the reasons behind this phenomenon and provides practical advice on how to prioritize experiential spending.

The Happiness of Experiences

Experiences, such as travel, concerts, dining out, and participating in recreational activities, offer unique and enduring benefits that material possessions often cannot match. Here are some key reasons why experiences tend to lead to greater happiness:

1. Enduring Memories: Experiences create lasting memories that individuals can recall and cherish for years. These memories contribute to long-term happiness and can be revisited mentally, providing joy and satisfaction.

2. Social Connections: Many experiences involve interacting with others, whether it's family, friends, or new acquaintances. These social interactions strengthen relationships and foster a sense of belonging, both of which are crucial for well-being.

3. Personal Growth: Engaging in new and diverse experiences promotes personal growth and self-improvement. Trying new activities, learning new skills, and exploring different cultures can enhance one's sense of accomplishment and purpose.

4. Reduced Hedonic Adaptation: Unlike material possessions, which quickly become part of the background of everyday life, experiences are less subject to hedonic adaptation. The novelty and emotional richness of experiences help maintain their positive impact on happiness over time.

5. Intrinsic Value: Experiences often align with intrinsic values such as personal development, relationships, and meaningful engagement. These values are more strongly

associated with long-term happiness than extrinsic values like status and wealth.

The Limitations of Material Possessions

While material possessions can provide temporary pleasure and convenience, they often fall short in delivering sustained happiness. Here are some reasons why possessions may not contribute to long-term well-being:

1. Hedonic Adaptation: People quickly adapt to new possessions, leading to a decline in the initial excitement and happiness they provide. This adaptation prompts a continuous cycle of acquiring new items without achieving lasting satisfaction.

2. Social Comparison: Material possessions are often used as a basis for social comparison. Comparing oneself to others based on possessions can lead to feelings of inadequacy, envy, and lower self-esteem.

3. Clutter and Maintenance: Accumulating possessions can result in clutter and the burden of maintenance, which can cause stress and reduce overall well-being. Managing and organizing a large number of items can be time-consuming and mentally taxing.

4. Financial Strain: Excessive spending on material goods can lead to financial strain and debt, causing stress and

anxiety. Financial insecurity negatively impacts mental and physical health, undermining happiness.

Research Findings on Experiential Spending

Numerous studies have examined the impact of experiential versus material spending on happiness. Some key findings include:

1. Anticipation and Planning: Anticipating and planning experiences can enhance happiness even before the experience occurs. The excitement and positive emotions associated with looking forward to an experience contribute to overall well-being.

2. Social Bonding: Shared experiences with others strengthen social bonds and create a sense of community. These connections are vital for emotional support and life satisfaction.

3. Sense of Identity: Experiences often become part of one's identity and contribute to a sense of self. People are more likely to define themselves by their experiences than by their possessions, which enhances self-worth and happiness.

4. Memory and Storytelling: Experiences generate stories and memories that people enjoy sharing with others. These stories reinforce positive emotions and create a sense of continuity and meaning in life.

Practical Advice for Prioritizing Experiential Spending

Shifting focus from material possessions to experiences requires intentional effort and planning. Here are some practical strategies to help prioritize experiential spending:

1. Set Experiential Goals: Identify and set goals related to experiences you want to have. This could include travel destinations, cultural events, personal development activities, or new hobbies. Setting clear goals helps prioritize spending and plan for meaningful experiences.

2. Create a Budget for Experiences: Allocate a specific portion of your budget for experiences. This ensures that you have the financial resources to invest in activities that bring joy and fulfillment. Consider cutting back on unnecessary material purchases to free up funds for experiences.

3. Plan and Schedule Experiences: Plan experiences in advance and schedule them into your calendar. Whether it's a weekend getaway, a concert, or a cooking class, having planned activities ensures you make time for experiences and look forward to them.

4. Embrace Minimalism: Adopt a minimalist approach to possessions by decluttering and simplifying your life. Focus on quality over quantity and invest in items that truly add

value to your life. This creates space for more meaningful experiences.

5. Involve Others: Share experiences with friends and family to enhance social connections and create lasting memories. Planning group activities or trips can strengthen relationships and make experiences more enjoyable.

6. Reflect on Experiences: Take time to reflect on and savor your experiences. Keep a journal, create photo albums, or share stories with others to reinforce positive memories and emotions.

7. Gift Experiences: Instead of giving material gifts, consider giving experiences to others. This could include tickets to events, vouchers for activities, or planned outings. Experiential gifts often provide more lasting joy and appreciation.

8. Prioritize Learning and Growth: Invest in experiences that promote personal growth and learning. This could include workshops, classes, and educational trips. Personal development experiences contribute to a sense of accomplishment and fulfillment.

9. Focus on Health and Well-Being: Prioritize experiences that enhance your physical and mental health, such as fitness activities, outdoor adventures, and relaxation

retreats. These activities contribute to overall well-being and happiness.

Overcoming Barriers to Experiential Spending

While the benefits of experiential spending are clear, some individuals may face barriers to prioritizing experiences over possessions. Common barriers and strategies to overcome them include:

1. Financial Constraints: Limited financial resources can make it challenging to invest in experiences. Look for low-cost or free experiences, such as hiking, visiting local museums, or attending community events. Saving gradually for larger experiences can also make them more attainable.

2. Time Constraints: Busy schedules and responsibilities can limit the time available for experiences. Prioritize experiences that fit within your schedule, such as weekend activities or short trips. Make intentional choices to carve out time for meaningful experiences.

3. Social Norms: Societal pressures and norms may emphasize material success and possessions. Surround yourself with like-minded individuals who value experiences and support your priorities. Focus on personal values rather than external expectations.

4. Habitual Spending: Habitual spending on material goods can be hard to break. Start by gradually shifting

spending habits and making conscious choices to invest in experiences. Reflect on the long-term benefits of experiences to reinforce new habits.

Spending money on experiences rather than possessions leads to greater happiness and life satisfaction. Experiences create lasting memories, strengthen social connections, promote personal growth, and reduce the negative impacts of hedonic adaptation and social comparison. By prioritizing experiential spending and overcoming barriers, individuals can enhance their well-being and lead more fulfilling lives.

CHAPTER 09

FINANCIAL STRESS AND MENTAL HEALTH

Financial stress is a pervasive issue that affects people across various socio-economic backgrounds. It is a significant contributor to mental health problems such as anxiety, depression, and other stress-related disorders. Understanding the impact of financial stress on well-being and learning how to manage and reduce financial anxiety are crucial steps toward achieving better mental health and overall happiness. This chapter explores the relationship between financial stress and mental health and provides practical strategies for managing financial anxiety.

The Impact of Financial Stress on Mental Health

Financial stress arises from concerns about money, debt, income, and financial security. It can manifest in various ways, including:

1. Anxiety: Constant worry about finances can lead to anxiety, characterized by feelings of nervousness, restlessness, and fear. This anxiety can interfere with daily activities and overall well-being.

2. Depression: Persistent financial stress can contribute to depression, marked by feelings of hopelessness, sadness, and a lack of interest in activities once enjoyed. Depression can severely impact an individual's quality of life.

3. Sleep Disorders: Financial worries often lead to sleep disturbances, such as insomnia or restless sleep. Lack of sleep can exacerbate stress and negatively affect physical and mental health.

4. Physical Health Problems: Chronic stress from financial issues can lead to physical health problems, including headaches, high blood pressure, gastrointestinal issues, and weakened immune function.

5. Relationship Strain: Financial stress can strain relationships with family and friends, leading to conflicts, reduced communication, and feelings of isolation.

6. Reduced Cognitive Function: High levels of stress can impair cognitive functions such as decision-making, concentration, and memory. This can further complicate financial management and create a vicious cycle of stress and poor financial decisions.

Causes of Financial Stress

Understanding the common causes of financial stress can help individuals identify their specific stressors and address them effectively. Some common causes include:

1. Debt: High levels of debt, including credit card debt, student loans, and mortgages, are major sources of financial stress. The burden of repayments and interest can create significant anxiety.

2. Income Instability: Unstable or insufficient income, including irregular work schedules, freelance or gig work, and job insecurity, can cause ongoing financial worries.

3. Living Expenses: Rising living costs, including housing, utilities, healthcare, and education, can strain budgets and create financial stress.

4. Unexpected Expenses: Unplanned expenses, such as medical emergencies, car repairs, or home maintenance, can disrupt financial stability and cause anxiety.

5. Lack of Savings: Insufficient savings or emergency funds can leave individuals vulnerable to financial shocks and increase stress about the future.

6. Financial Illiteracy: A lack of financial knowledge and skills can lead to poor money management, exacerbating financial stress.

Strategies for Managing and Reducing Financial Anxiety

Managing financial stress involves both practical financial management strategies and psychological techniques to cope with stress. Here are some effective strategies for reducing financial anxiety:

1. Create a Budget: Developing a detailed budget helps track income and expenses, providing a clear picture of your financial situation. A budget can identify areas where you can cut costs and allocate funds more effectively.

2. Build an Emergency Fund: Establishing an emergency fund provides a financial safety net for unexpected expenses. Aim to save three to six months' worth of living expenses to reduce financial vulnerability.

3. Reduce Debt: Develop a plan to pay down debt systematically. Focus on high-interest debt first and consider strategies such as debt consolidation or negotiating lower interest rates with creditors.

4. Increase Financial Literacy: Educate yourself about personal finance through books, online resources, and financial literacy courses. Understanding financial concepts can empower you to make better financial decisions.

5. Seek Professional Advice: Consider consulting a financial advisor or credit counselor for personalized advice

and guidance. Professional support can help you develop a realistic financial plan and address specific concerns.

6. Practice Mindfulness and Stress Reduction Techniques: Mindfulness practices, such as meditation, deep breathing exercises, and yoga, can help manage stress and improve mental well-being. Regular physical activity and adequate sleep are also essential for reducing stress.

7. Set Realistic Goals: Establish achievable financial goals and break them down into smaller, manageable steps. Celebrate progress toward these goals to maintain motivation and reduce anxiety.

8. Develop a Positive Money Mindset: Cultivate a positive attitude toward money by focusing on what you can control and practicing gratitude for what you have. Reframe negative thoughts about money and challenge limiting beliefs.

9. Communicate Openly: If financial stress is affecting your relationships, communicate openly with your partner, family, or friends. Working together to address financial challenges can strengthen relationships and reduce feelings of isolation.

10. Limit Social Comparison: Avoid comparing your financial situation to others, as this can exacerbate stress and dissatisfaction. Focus on your own financial goals and progress.

Case Studies: Real-Life Examples

Examining real-life examples of individuals who have successfully managed financial stress can provide valuable insights and inspiration. Here are a few case studies:

1. Sarah's Debt Reduction Journey: Sarah accumulated significant credit card debt during her college years. Overwhelmed by her financial situation, she sought the help of a credit counselor who helped her create a debt repayment plan. By sticking to a budget, cutting unnecessary expenses, and making consistent payments, Sarah gradually paid off her debt and built an emergency fund. Her financial stress decreased, and she felt more in control of her future.

2. John's Income Stability Plan: John worked as a freelance graphic designer with an irregular income. To manage financial stress, he diversified his income streams by taking on part-time work and creating passive income sources, such as selling digital products. He also built a larger emergency fund to cover periods of low income. These steps provided greater financial stability and reduced his anxiety about the future.

3. Maria's Mindfulness Practice: Maria experienced financial stress due to high living expenses and student loans. She began practicing mindfulness and meditation to manage her anxiety. Maria also attended financial literacy workshops

to improve her money management skills. By combining practical financial strategies with mindfulness techniques, she significantly reduced her financial stress and improved her overall well-being.

Seeking Support for Financial Stress

If financial stress becomes overwhelming and starts to impact your mental health severely, it's essential to seek support. Here are some resources that can help:

1. Therapists and Counselors: Mental health professionals can provide support for managing stress, anxiety, and depression related to financial issues. Cognitive-behavioral therapy (CBT) is particularly effective in addressing negative thought patterns and behaviors.

2. Financial Advisors and Credit Counselors: Financial professionals can offer personalized advice and strategies for managing debt, budgeting, and saving. They can help you develop a comprehensive financial plan to reduce stress.

3. Support Groups: Joining support groups for individuals facing similar financial challenges can provide a sense of community and shared understanding. These groups can offer practical tips and emotional support.

4. Online Resources and Tools: Numerous online resources, including budgeting apps, financial planning tools,

and educational websites, can help you manage your finances and reduce stress.

Financial stress is a significant contributor to mental health issues, but it can be managed and reduced with the right strategies and support. By understanding the impact of financial stress on well-being and implementing practical financial management techniques, individuals can achieve greater financial stability and improve their mental health. Combining these strategies with mindfulness practices and seeking professional support when needed can help mitigate the negative effects of financial stress and lead to a more balanced and fulfilling life.

CHAPTER 10

GENEROSITY AND ALTRUISM

Generosity and altruism are powerful behaviors that have the potential to significantly boost happiness and well-being. Acts of giving, whether through time, resources, or kindness, can create a profound sense of purpose and fulfillment. This chapter explores the psychological benefits of generosity and altruism, examining how helping others enhances our own happiness and contributes to a more meaningful life.

The Psychological Benefits of Generosity

Generosity, the act of giving freely without expecting anything in return, is associated with numerous psychological benefits. These benefits not only enhance the well-being of those who receive but also significantly impact the givers. Here are some key psychological benefits of generosity:

1. Increased Happiness: Research consistently shows that generous individuals experience higher levels of happiness. Acts of giving activate the brain's reward system, releasing feel-good chemicals such as dopamine, which contribute to a sense of joy and satisfaction.

2. Enhanced Sense of Purpose: Generosity helps individuals find meaning and purpose in their lives. Helping others fosters a sense of connection and contribution, making people feel that their actions have a positive impact on the world.

3. Improved Mental Health: Engaging in altruistic behaviors can reduce symptoms of depression and anxiety. The focus shifts from one's own problems to the needs of others, providing a sense of perspective and reducing feelings of isolation.

4. Greater Life Satisfaction: Generous people often report higher levels of life satisfaction. The act of giving creates a sense of fulfillment and contentment that material possessions alone cannot provide.

5. Stronger Social Connections: Generosity fosters social bonds and strengthens relationships. Helping others builds trust, empathy, and mutual support, which are crucial for emotional well-being.

6. Lower Stress Levels: Acts of generosity can reduce stress by promoting positive emotions and reducing the physiological effects of stress. Helping others can lead to lower blood pressure and a stronger immune system.

The Science Behind Altruism

Altruism, the selfless concern for the well-being of others, is deeply rooted in human psychology and biology. Evolutionary theories suggest that altruism has been crucial for the survival and thriving of human societies. Here are some scientific explanations for why altruism benefits both individuals and communities:

1. Biological Basis: Altruistic behavior is linked to the release of oxytocin, a hormone associated with bonding and social connections. Oxytocin promotes feelings of trust, empathy, and generosity, reinforcing altruistic actions.

2. Evolutionary Advantage: Altruism has evolutionary advantages as it promotes group cohesion and cooperation. Helping others increases the chances of survival for the group, which in turn benefits the individual.

3. Reciprocal Altruism: The concept of reciprocal altruism suggests that individuals are more likely to help others if they believe the favor will be returned in the future. This creates a cycle of mutual support and cooperation.

4. Social and Cultural Factors: Cultural norms and socialization play a significant role in promoting altruistic behavior. Societies that value generosity and community support tend to have higher levels of well-being and social harmony.

How Helping Others Enhances Personal Fulfillment

Helping others provides a unique sense of fulfillment that material pursuits often fail to deliver. Here are some ways in which altruism contributes to personal fulfillment:

1. Positive Identity: Engaging in altruistic behaviors helps individuals develop a positive self-identity. Seeing oneself as a kind and generous person boosts self-esteem and self-worth.

2. Meaningful Relationships: Altruism fosters deeper and more meaningful relationships. Acts of kindness create a sense of reciprocity and trust, leading to stronger and more supportive social networks.

3. Gratitude and Perspective: Helping others cultivates a sense of gratitude and perspective. It reminds individuals of their own blessings and reduces feelings of entitlement and dissatisfaction.

4. Emotional Resilience: Altruistic individuals tend to be more emotionally resilient. The positive emotions

generated by helping others can buffer against stress and adversity, enhancing overall mental health.

5. Spiritual Growth: For many, acts of generosity are closely tied to spiritual and moral values. Altruism can lead to spiritual growth and a deeper sense of connection to a higher purpose or calling.

Practical Ways to Cultivate Generosity

Cultivating generosity requires intentional effort and a shift in mindset. Here are some practical ways to incorporate altruism into daily life:

1. Volunteer Your Time: Volunteering is a powerful way to give back to the community. Whether it's at a local shelter, hospital, or school, dedicating time to help others creates a sense of purpose and fulfillment.

2. Donate to Causes You Care About: Financial contributions to charities and organizations that align with your values can make a significant impact. Research and choose causes that resonate with you and support them regularly.

3. Perform Random Acts of Kindness: Simple acts of kindness, such as paying for someone's coffee, helping a neighbor, or offering a kind word, can brighten someone's day and enhance your own happiness.

4. Share Your Skills and Talents: Use your unique skills and talents to benefit others. Whether it's tutoring, mentoring, or offering professional services pro bono, sharing your expertise can be incredibly rewarding.

5. Practice Empathy and Compassion: Cultivate empathy and compassion by actively listening to others and showing understanding and support. Empathy strengthens social connections and fosters a sense of community.

6. Create a Giving Plan: Establish a giving plan that outlines your goals for charitable contributions and volunteer activities. Having a structured approach to generosity ensures consistent and meaningful giving.

Overcoming Barriers to Generosity

While generosity has numerous benefits, some individuals may face barriers that prevent them from giving. Here are common obstacles and strategies to overcome them:

1. Financial Constraints: Financial limitations can make monetary donations challenging. Focus on non-monetary ways to give, such as volunteering time, offering skills, or providing emotional support.

2. Time Constraints: Busy schedules can hinder the ability to volunteer. Look for flexible volunteer opportunities that fit your schedule or consider micro-volunteering, which involves short, impactful activities.

3. Skepticism and Trust Issues: Concerns about the effectiveness of charities can deter giving. Research organizations thoroughly and choose those with transparency and a proven track record of impact.

4. Emotional Burnout: Constantly giving without self-care can lead to burnout. Balance generosity with self-care and set healthy boundaries to maintain your well-being.

5. Fear of Judgment: Some individuals fear judgment or criticism for their acts of generosity. Focus on the positive impact of your actions and surround yourself with supportive people who share your values.

Generosity and altruism have profound psychological benefits that enhance happiness and well-being. Acts of giving create a sense of purpose, strengthen social connections, and improve mental health. By understanding the science behind altruism and incorporating practical ways to cultivate generosity, individuals can experience greater fulfillment and contribute positively to their communities.

CHAPTER 11

MONEY, RELATIONSHIPS, AND SOCIAL CONNECTIONS

Relationships and social connections are integral to happiness and well-being. The role of money in these relationships can be both positive and negative, impacting social ties in various ways. This chapter explores how money influences relationships and social connections, offering insights and practical tips for maintaining healthy relationships regardless of financial status.

The Importance of Relationships and Social Connections

Social connections are essential for emotional support, personal growth, and overall well-being. Strong relationships with family, friends, and community members provide a sense of belonging and purpose, significantly contributing to life satisfaction. Key benefits of social connections include:

1. Emotional Support: Relationships provide a network of emotional support, helping individuals navigate life's challenges and celebrate successes.

2. Mental Health: Social connections reduce feelings of loneliness and isolation, decreasing the risk of depression and anxiety.

3. Physical Health: Studies show that individuals with strong social ties have better physical health, including lower blood pressure, reduced risk of chronic diseases, and increased longevity.

4. Personal Growth: Relationships offer opportunities for personal growth through shared experiences, learning, and mutual support.

How Money Influences Relationships

Money can have a profound impact on relationships, influencing them in both positive and negative ways. Understanding these dynamics is crucial for maintaining healthy social connections.

Positive Influences of Money on Relationships:

1. Providing Stability: Financial stability can reduce stress and create a secure environment for relationships to flourish. It allows for the fulfillment of basic needs and the ability to support loved ones.

2. Enabling Shared Experiences: Money can facilitate shared experiences, such as vacations, dining out, and recreational activities, which strengthen bonds and create lasting memories.

3. Supporting Others: Financial resources enable individuals to help friends and family in need, fostering a sense of community and mutual support.

Negative Influences of Money on Relationships:

1. Financial Stress: Financial difficulties can strain relationships, leading to conflicts, misunderstandings, and emotional stress. Money-related arguments are a common source of tension in relationships.

2. Power Imbalances: Disparities in income and financial control can create power imbalances, leading to feelings of resentment, dependence, or inequality within relationships.

3. Materialism: An excessive focus on material wealth can overshadow the importance of relationships, leading to superficial connections and reduced life satisfaction.

Money and Romantic Relationships

Financial issues are a significant factor in romantic relationships, impacting everything from daily interactions to long-term commitments. Key areas of influence include:

1. Financial Compatibility: Differences in financial values, spending habits, and financial goals can lead to conflicts in romantic relationships. Open communication about finances is essential for compatibility.

2. Joint Financial Planning: Couples who plan their finances together, set mutual goals, and manage joint accounts often experience greater relationship satisfaction and stability.

3. Debt and Savings: Managing debt and building savings as a team can strengthen relationships, fostering a sense of partnership and shared responsibility.

Tips for Healthy Financial Communication in Romantic Relationships:

1. Open Dialogue: Have regular and honest conversations about finances, including income, expenses, debts, and financial goals. Transparency builds trust and understanding.

2. Set Joint Goals: Establish joint financial goals and work together to achieve them. This creates a sense of teamwork and shared purpose.

3. Respect Differences: Acknowledge and respect each other's financial values and habits. Compromise and find common ground to avoid conflicts.

4. Seek Professional Advice: Consider consulting a financial advisor to help navigate complex financial issues and develop a joint financial plan.

Money and Family Relationships

Financial dynamics within families can be complex, affecting relationships between parents and children, siblings, and extended family members. Key considerations include:

1. Supporting Dependents: Financially supporting children, elderly parents, or other dependents can create stress but also strengthen family bonds through care and responsibility.

2. Inheritance and Estate Planning: Discussions about inheritance and estate planning can be sensitive but are crucial for preventing conflicts and ensuring fair distribution of assets.

3. Financial Education: Teaching children about money management and financial responsibility fosters independence and prepares them for future financial challenges.

Tips for Healthy Financial Relationships in Families:

1. Communicate Clearly: Discuss financial expectations, responsibilities, and plans openly with family members to prevent misunderstandings and conflicts.

2. Encourage Independence: Foster financial independence in children and other family members by providing guidance and support without creating dependency.

3. Plan for the Future: Engage in estate planning and discuss inheritance openly to ensure clarity and prevent disputes.

4. Provide Financial Education: Educate family members about financial management, budgeting, and saving to promote financial literacy and responsibility.

Money and Friendships

Friendships are another area where money can play a significant role, influencing social interactions and the quality of connections. Key aspects include:

1. Social Activities: Money can affect the ability to participate in social activities, leading to feelings of exclusion or financial pressure to keep up with friends' spending.

2. Lending and Borrowing: Financial transactions between friends, such as lending and borrowing money, can create tension and strain relationships if not handled carefully.

3. Status and Comparison: Differences in financial status can lead to social comparison, jealousy, or feelings of inadequacy, impacting the quality of friendships.

Tips for Healthy Financial Relationships with Friends:

1. Set Boundaries: Establish clear boundaries when it comes to lending and borrowing money. Communicate openly about expectations and repayment terms.

2. Be Inclusive: Choose social activities that are inclusive and considerate of friends' financial situations. Opt for low-cost or free activities to ensure everyone can participate.

3. Avoid Comparison: Focus on the quality of friendships rather than financial status. Avoid comparing your financial situation to that of your friends.

4. Offer Support: Provide emotional and practical support to friends facing financial difficulties without judgment or pressure.

Building and Maintaining Healthy Social Connections

Regardless of financial status, building and maintaining healthy social connections is crucial for happiness and well-being. Here are some strategies to foster strong relationships:

1. Prioritize Relationships: Make time for family, friends, and community. Invest in relationships by spending quality time together and engaging in meaningful activities.

2. Communicate Effectively: Open and honest communication is key to maintaining healthy relationships.

Share your thoughts, feelings, and concerns openly and listen actively to others.

3. Show Appreciation: Express gratitude and appreciation for the people in your life. Small gestures of kindness and acknowledgment go a long way in strengthening bonds.

4. Be Supportive: Offer emotional support and practical help to loved ones in times of need. Being there for others fosters trust and deepens connections.

5. Practice Empathy: Understand and empathize with others' perspectives and experiences. Empathy builds stronger, more compassionate relationships.

Money plays a significant role in relationships and social connections, influencing them in various ways. While financial stability can enhance relationships by providing security and enabling shared experiences, financial stress and disparities can create tension and strain. By understanding the dynamics of money in relationships and practicing effective communication, empathy, and financial management, individuals can build and maintain healthy social ties regardless of their financial status.

CHAPTER 12

THE ROLE OF CULTURE AND SOCIETY

Cultural and societal factors profoundly shape the relationship between money and happiness. Different cultures have distinct attitudes toward wealth and well-being, and societal norms can significantly influence individual happiness. This chapter explores various cultural perspectives on wealth and well-being and examines how societal norms impact individual happiness.

Cultural Perspectives on Wealth and Well-Being

Cultures around the world have diverse beliefs and practices regarding wealth and well-being. These cultural perspectives influence how individuals perceive and pursue happiness.

Western Cultures:

1. Individualism and Materialism: Western cultures, particularly in the United States and Western Europe, often

emphasize individualism and material success. Wealth is frequently seen as a measure of personal achievement and a source of social status. The pursuit of material possessions and financial success is deeply ingrained in societal values.

2. Work Ethic: The Protestant work ethic, prevalent in many Western cultures, promotes the idea that hard work and economic success are virtuous and lead to personal fulfillment. This cultural norm can drive individuals to prioritize their careers and financial goals.

Eastern Cultures:

1. Collectivism and Harmony: In contrast, many Eastern cultures, such as those in East Asia, emphasize collectivism and social harmony. Wealth is often viewed in the context of family and community well-being rather than individual achievement. Social relationships and communal support are highly valued.

2. Spirituality and Moderation: Eastern philosophies, such as Buddhism and Confucianism, often promote spiritual growth and moderation over material accumulation. The pursuit of inner peace and balance is considered essential for well-being.

Indigenous Cultures:

1. Community and Sustainability: Indigenous cultures around the world, including Native American, Aboriginal

Australian, and various African tribes, often prioritize community well-being and sustainable living. Wealth is typically measured in terms of resources shared within the community and the ability to live in harmony with nature.

2. Cultural Traditions: Traditional practices and cultural heritage play a significant role in defining well-being in indigenous cultures. The preservation of cultural identity and practices is often seen as more important than material wealth.

Societal Norms and Individual Happiness

Societal norms, or the shared expectations and rules that guide behavior in a society, greatly influence individual happiness. These norms shape attitudes toward wealth, success, and well-being.

Consumer Culture:

1. Material Wealth and Status: In societies with strong consumer cultures, material wealth and the acquisition of possessions are often seen as indicators of success and happiness. Advertising and media reinforce the idea that happiness can be bought, leading individuals to prioritize consumption.

2. Social Comparison: Consumer culture promotes social comparison, where individuals measure their success and happiness against others based on material possessions.

This can lead to feelings of inadequacy and dissatisfaction, even among those who are relatively well-off.

Economic Inequality:

1. Income Disparity: High levels of income inequality within a society can negatively impact overall happiness. When wealth is concentrated in the hands of a few, it can lead to social tensions, reduced trust, and increased stress among those with lower incomes.

2. Social Mobility: Societies with low social mobility, where individuals have limited opportunities to improve their economic status, often experience lower levels of happiness. The perception that hard work and talent do not lead to better outcomes can lead to frustration and hopelessness.

Work-Life Balance:

1. Cultural Expectations: Societal norms around work and leisure significantly affect happiness. In cultures where long working hours and career success are highly valued, individuals may experience higher stress levels and less satisfaction with life.

2. Policy Support: Societies with policies that support work-life balance, such as generous parental leave, flexible work arrangements, and vacation time, tend to have higher levels of happiness. These policies allow individuals to balance their professional and personal lives more effectively.

Social Support and Community:

1. Community Engagement: Societies that encourage community engagement and social support networks tend to have higher levels of happiness. Strong social ties and a sense of belonging contribute significantly to well-being.

2. Public Services: Access to quality public services, such as healthcare, education, and social security, enhances happiness by providing security and reducing stress. Societies that invest in public welfare generally report higher levels of life satisfaction.

Case Studies: Cultural Influences on Happiness

Examining specific countries and cultures can provide deeper insights into how cultural and societal factors influence happiness.

Denmark:

Denmark consistently ranks high on global happiness indexes. Key factors contributing to Danish happiness include:

1. Work-Life Balance: Danish culture values work-life balance, with policies supporting flexible work hours, parental leave, and ample vacation time.

2. Social Welfare: Denmark's comprehensive social welfare system provides healthcare, education, and financial security, reducing stress and promoting well-being.

3. Community and Trust: High levels of social trust and community engagement foster a sense of belonging and mutual support.

Japan:

Japan presents a complex picture of happiness, influenced by both positive and negative cultural factors:

1. Social Harmony: Japanese culture emphasizes social harmony, respect, and community, contributing to strong social ties and a sense of belonging.

2. Work Culture: However, Japan's demanding work culture, characterized by long hours and high stress, can negatively impact happiness. Efforts to improve work-life balance are ongoing.

Bhutan:

Bhutan measures success through Gross National Happiness (GNH) rather than Gross Domestic Product (GDP). Key elements of Bhutanese happiness include:

1. Cultural Preservation: Bhutan places a high value on cultural preservation, spiritual well-being, and environmental sustainability.

2. Community and Family: Strong community ties and family support are central to Bhutanese life, enhancing social cohesion and happiness.

Practical Tips for Navigating Cultural and Societal Influences

Regardless of cultural and societal norms, individuals can take proactive steps to enhance their happiness:

1. Align with Personal Values: Identify and prioritize personal values that contribute to happiness, such as relationships, personal growth, and community involvement, regardless of societal pressures.

2. Seek Balance: Strive for a balance between work and personal life. Set boundaries and prioritize time for leisure, family, and self-care.

3. Cultivate Social Connections: Invest in building and maintaining strong social connections. Engage in community activities and support networks to foster a sense of belonging.

4. Practice Gratitude: Focus on the positive aspects of life and practice gratitude regularly. Recognize and appreciate the non-material aspects of well-being.

5. Advocate for Change: Support policies and initiatives that promote social welfare, economic equality, and work-life balance. Advocacy can lead to societal changes that enhance collective well-being.

Cultural and societal factors play a significant role in shaping the relationship between money and happiness. Different cultural perspectives on wealth and well-being, along with societal norms, influence individual happiness in various ways. By understanding these influences and taking proactive steps to align personal values with cultural and societal contexts, individuals can navigate the complex interplay between wealth and well-being.

CHAPTER 13

FINANCIAL MANAGEMENT AND HAPPINESS

Effective financial management is essential for reducing stress, achieving financial stability, and enhancing overall happiness. By taking control of your finances through budgeting, saving, investing, and planning for the future, you can create a more secure and fulfilling life. This chapter provides practical advice on managing your finances to boost your well-being.

The Importance of Financial Management

Financial management involves making informed decisions about how to use and allocate your financial resources. It encompasses various aspects, including budgeting, saving, investing, and planning for the future. Effective financial management offers several key benefits:

1. Reduced Stress: Managing finances effectively can alleviate the stress and anxiety associated with financial uncertainty and debt.

2. Increased Control: Having a clear financial plan gives you a sense of control over your financial future, contributing to greater peace of mind.

3. Enhanced Security: Financial management helps build a safety net for emergencies and future needs, providing financial security.

4. Goal Achievement: Setting and achieving financial goals enhances satisfaction and a sense of accomplishment.

5. Improved Relationships: Clear financial management reduces money-related conflicts in relationships, fostering harmony and trust.

Budgeting: The Foundation of Financial Management

Budgeting is the cornerstone of effective financial management. It involves tracking your income and expenses to ensure that you live within your means and allocate resources to meet your financial goals.

Steps to Create an Effective Budget:

1. Track Income and Expenses: Start by tracking all sources of income and recording all expenses over a month. This will give you a clear picture of your financial situation.

2. Categorize Expenses: Divide your expenses into categories, such as housing, utilities, groceries, transportation, entertainment, and savings.

3. Set Priorities: Identify essential expenses and discretionary spending. Prioritize needs over wants to ensure that you cover essential expenses first.

4. Set Financial Goals: Define short-term and long-term financial goals, such as saving for a vacation, paying off debt, or building an emergency fund.

5. Create a Spending Plan: Allocate your income to different expense categories based on your priorities and goals. Ensure that your total expenses do not exceed your income.

6. Monitor and Adjust: Regularly review your budget to track progress and make adjustments as needed. Be flexible and willing to adapt to changes in your financial situation.

Tips for Successful Budgeting:

- Use Budgeting Tools: Utilize budgeting apps or spreadsheets to simplify tracking and managing your finances.

- Automate Savings: Set up automatic transfers to savings accounts to ensure consistent saving without relying on willpower.

- Limit Impulse Spending: Avoid impulsive purchases by creating a waiting period for non-essential items. This helps you make more intentional spending decisions.

- Review and Reflect: Regularly review your budget and reflect on your spending habits. Identify areas for improvement and celebrate progress toward your goals.

Saving: Building Financial Security

Saving is a critical component of financial management that provides a safety net for emergencies and future needs. Building savings enhances financial security and reduces stress.

Types of Savings:

1. Emergency Fund: An emergency fund is a savings account designated for unexpected expenses, such as medical emergencies, car repairs, or job loss. Aim to save three to six months' worth of living expenses.

2. Short-Term Savings: Short-term savings are for goals you plan to achieve within the next one to five years, such as a vacation, home down payment, or major purchase.

3. Long-Term Savings: Long-term savings are for future financial goals, such as retirement, education expenses, or major investments.

Strategies for Effective Saving:

- Pay Yourself First: Treat savings as a non-negotiable expense by setting aside a portion of your income for savings before paying other bills.

- Automate Savings: Automate contributions to savings accounts to ensure consistent saving without the need for manual transfers.

- Cut Unnecessary Expenses: Identify and reduce discretionary spending to free up more funds for savings.

- Use High-Interest Accounts: Utilize high-interest savings accounts or certificates of deposit (CDs) to maximize the growth of your savings.

Investing: Growing Wealth for the Future

Investing involves putting your money into financial assets with the goal of growing wealth over time. It is essential for achieving long-term financial goals and building a secure financial future.

Types of Investments:

1. Stocks: Investing in stocks involves buying shares of publicly traded companies. Stocks offer the potential for high returns but come with higher risk.

2. Bonds: Bonds are debt securities issued by governments or corporations. They provide regular interest payments and are generally considered lower risk than stocks.

3. Mutual Funds: Mutual funds pool money from multiple investors to invest in a diversified portfolio of stocks, bonds, or other assets. They offer diversification and professional management.

4. Real Estate: Investing in real estate involves purchasing property for rental income or capital appreciation. Real estate can provide steady income and potential tax benefits.

5. Retirement Accounts: Retirement accounts, such as 401(k)s and IRAs, offer tax advantages and are designed to help you save for retirement.

Strategies for Successful Investing:

- Start Early: The earlier you start investing, the more time your money has to grow through compounding. Even small contributions can grow significantly over time.

- Diversify: Diversify your investments to spread risk and increase the potential for returns. Avoid putting all your money into a single asset or investment type.

- Understand Risk Tolerance: Assess your risk tolerance and choose investments that align with your comfort level. Higher-risk investments can offer higher returns but may not be suitable for everyone.

- Educate Yourself: Educate yourself about different investment options and strategies. Understanding the basics of investing can help you make informed decisions.

- Seek Professional Advice: Consider consulting a financial advisor for personalized investment advice and strategies. A professional can help you develop a diversified investment portfolio tailored to your goals.

Planning for the Future: Setting and Achieving Financial Goals

Financial planning involves setting clear financial goals and developing a roadmap to achieve them. Effective financial planning provides direction and motivation, enhancing overall happiness and well-being.

Steps for Effective Financial Planning:

1. Define Financial Goals: Identify specific, measurable, achievable, relevant, and time-bound (SMART) financial goals. Examples include saving for a home, paying off debt, funding education, or retiring comfortably.

2. Assess Your Current Situation: Evaluate your current financial situation, including income, expenses, assets, liabilities, and net worth. Understanding your starting point is essential for effective planning.

3. Develop a Plan: Create a detailed plan to achieve your financial goals. Outline the steps, timeline, and resources needed to reach each goal.

4. Implement the Plan: Put your financial plan into action by making necessary changes to your spending, saving, and investing habits.

5. Monitor Progress: Regularly review your financial plan and track your progress toward your goals. Make adjustments as needed to stay on track.

6. Celebrate Milestones: Celebrate achieving financial milestones to stay motivated and acknowledge your progress.

Tips for Successful Financial Planning:

- Be Realistic: Set realistic and achievable goals based on your financial situation and resources.

- Stay Flexible: Be willing to adapt your plan as circumstances change. Flexibility is essential for navigating unexpected challenges and opportunities.

- Prioritize Goals: Focus on achieving high-priority goals first, such as building an emergency fund or paying off high-interest debt.

- Seek Guidance: Consider working with a financial planner or advisor to develop a comprehensive financial plan tailored to your needs.

Effective financial management is crucial for reducing stress, achieving financial stability, and enhancing overall happiness. By budgeting, saving, investing, and planning for the future, individuals can take control of their finances and create a secure and fulfilling life. Implementing the strategies outlined in this chapter can help you navigate the complex world of personal finance and achieve greater well-being.

CHAPTER 14

CASE STUDIES: LESSONS FROM THE RICH AND THE POOR

Real-life case studies offer valuable insights into the complex relationship between money and happiness. By examining the experiences of individuals from different economic backgrounds, we can identify key lessons on achieving happiness regardless of financial status. This chapter presents stories from both wealthy and less affluent individuals, highlighting the diverse ways in which people find contentment and well-being.

Case Study 1: The Wealthy Entrepreneur

Background:

John is a successful entrepreneur who built a multi-million-dollar tech company from the ground up. His journey to wealth was marked by long hours, significant risks, and strategic decisions. Despite his financial success, John found himself struggling with happiness.

Challenges:

1. Work-Life Balance: John's relentless focus on his business led to a lack of balance in his personal life. Long hours and constant stress took a toll on his health and relationships.

2. Social Isolation: As his wealth grew, John felt increasingly isolated from friends and family who couldn't relate to his experiences and pressures.

3. Hedonic Adaptation: Despite his financial achievements, John found that the initial excitement of wealth quickly faded, leading to a constant pursuit of new goals and possessions.

Strategies for Happiness:

1. Prioritizing Relationships: John made a conscious effort to reconnect with family and friends, scheduling regular social activities and quality time with loved ones.

2. Pursuing Passion Projects: He began investing time in hobbies and passion projects unrelated to his business, such as music and travel, which brought him joy and fulfillment.

3. Giving Back: John established a foundation to support education and entrepreneurship in underserved

communities. This act of giving provided a sense of purpose and deep satisfaction.

Lessons Learned:

- Wealth alone does not guarantee happiness. Building and maintaining strong relationships and pursuing personal passions are essential for well-being.

- Giving back and helping others can provide a profound sense of purpose and fulfillment.

Case Study 2: The Middle-Class Family

Background:

Maria and Carlos are a middle-class couple with two children. Both work full-time jobs to support their family and maintain a comfortable lifestyle. Despite financial stability, they often felt stressed and dissatisfied.

Challenges:

1. Financial Stress: The couple faced constant pressure to manage expenses, save for their children's education, and plan for retirement.

2. Work-Life Balance: Balancing work responsibilities with family time was a persistent challenge, leading to feelings of guilt and exhaustion.

3. Material Expectations: Societal pressures to maintain a certain lifestyle and provide material possessions for their children added to their stress.

Strategies for Happiness:

1. Budgeting and Financial Planning: Maria and Carlos created a detailed budget and financial plan, prioritizing savings and cutting unnecessary expenses. This reduced their financial stress and provided a clearer path to their goals.

2. Quality Family Time: They made a conscious effort to prioritize family activities, such as game nights, outdoor adventures, and shared meals, which strengthened their bond and created lasting memories.

3. Mindfulness and Gratitude: The couple practiced mindfulness and gratitude, focusing on the positive aspects of their lives and appreciating what they had rather than constantly striving for more.

Lessons Learned:

- Effective financial management and planning can significantly reduce stress and enhance happiness.

- Prioritizing quality time with family and practicing gratitude can improve overall well-being and satisfaction.

Case Study 3: The Struggling Single Parent

Background:

Linda is a single mother working two part-time jobs to support her two children. Despite her financial struggles, Linda remains resilient and focused on providing a happy life for her family.

Challenges:

1. Financial Hardship: Linda's limited income made it difficult to cover basic expenses, leading to constant financial stress and uncertainty.

2. Time Constraints: Juggling work and parenting responsibilities left little time for self-care or personal pursuits.

3. Social Stigma: Linda faced social stigma and judgment for her financial situation, which affected her self-esteem and confidence.

Strategies for Happiness:

1. Community Support: Linda sought support from community resources, such as food banks, affordable childcare programs, and local charities. This assistance alleviated some of her financial burdens.

2. Building a Support Network: She developed a strong support network of friends, family, and neighbors who provided emotional support, childcare help, and companionship.

3. Finding Joy in Simple Pleasures: Linda focused on finding joy in simple, low-cost activities, such as spending time outdoors, cooking with her children, and engaging in creative projects.

Lessons Learned:

- Building a strong support network and seeking community resources can provide crucial assistance and emotional support during difficult times.

- Finding joy in simple, everyday activities can significantly enhance happiness, even in the face of financial hardship.

Case Study 4: The Retiree on a Fixed Income

Background:

Tom is a retiree living on a fixed pension and social security. While he no longer has a high income, Tom has managed to create a fulfilling and contented life in retirement.

Challenges:

1. Fixed Income: Living on a fixed income required careful budgeting and financial planning to ensure that essential expenses were covered.

2. Health Concerns: Aging brought health challenges that needed to be managed within his financial constraints.

3. Social Engagement: After retiring, Tom initially struggled with finding new ways to stay socially engaged and active.

Strategies for Happiness:

1. Budgeting and Frugality: Tom developed a detailed budget that prioritized essential expenses and included

modest savings for unexpected costs. He embraced a frugal lifestyle that focused on value and sustainability.

2. Active Lifestyle: He stayed physically active by participating in low-cost activities such as walking, gardening, and community fitness classes, which improved his health and well-being.

3. Volunteering and Social Activities: Tom volunteered at local organizations and joined social clubs, which provided a sense of purpose and opportunities for social interaction.

Lessons Learned:

- Effective budgeting and a frugal lifestyle can ensure financial stability and reduce stress, even on a fixed income.

- Staying active and socially engaged can significantly enhance happiness and quality of life in retirement.

Case Study 5: The Young Professional

Background:

Emma is a young professional in her early 30s, working in a high-pressure corporate job. She earns a substantial income but often feels overwhelmed and dissatisfied.

Challenges:

1. Work Stress: The demands of her job and long working hours contributed to high levels of stress and burnout.

2. Social Isolation: Emma's focus on her career left little time for socializing or maintaining relationships, leading to feelings of loneliness.

3. Lack of Fulfillment: Despite her financial success, Emma felt a lack of fulfillment and questioned the meaning and purpose of her work.

Strategies for Happiness:

1. Work-Life Balance: Emma made a conscious effort to establish a better work-life balance by setting boundaries, delegating tasks, and taking regular breaks.

2. Pursuing Passions: She explored personal interests and hobbies outside of work, such as painting and hiking, which provided a sense of fulfillment and relaxation.

3. Building Relationships: Emma prioritized reconnecting with friends and family and expanding her social circle through community events and networking groups.

Lessons Learned:

- Achieving work-life balance is crucial for reducing stress and enhancing overall happiness.

- Pursuing personal passions and hobbies can provide a sense of fulfillment and well-being beyond financial success.

- Building and maintaining strong relationships is essential for emotional support and life satisfaction.

These case studies illustrate that happiness is not solely dependent on financial status but is influenced by a variety of factors, including relationships, personal fulfillment, effective financial management, and community support. By learning from the experiences of individuals across different economic backgrounds, we can identify strategies to enhance happiness and well-being, regardless of our financial situation.

CHAPTER 15

STRATEGIES FOR ENHANCING FINANCIAL WELL-BEING

Financial well-being is a crucial component of overall happiness and quality of life. By adopting effective strategies for managing finances, individuals can reduce stress, achieve their financial goals, and enhance their overall well-being. This chapter compiles actionable strategies for improving financial well-being, focusing on financial literacy, goal setting, mindful spending, and seeking professional advice when necessary.

Financial Literacy: The Foundation of Financial Well-Being

Financial literacy is the ability to understand and effectively use various financial skills, including personal financial management, budgeting, and investing. Improving financial literacy is the first step toward enhancing financial well-being.

Key Areas of Financial Literacy:

1. Budgeting: Understanding how to create and maintain a budget is fundamental. A budget helps track income and expenses, ensuring that spending aligns with financial goals.

2. Saving and Investing: Knowing the importance of saving and the basics of investing helps build financial security and grow wealth over time.

3. Credit and Debt Management: Understanding how to use credit wisely and manage debt is crucial for maintaining financial health.

4. Financial Planning: Developing skills in financial planning allows individuals to set and achieve long-term financial goals, such as retirement planning, buying a home, or funding education.

Strategies to Improve Financial Literacy:

1. Educational Resources: Utilize books, online courses, and financial websites to learn about personal finance. Many resources are available for free or at low cost.

2. Workshops and Seminars: Attend financial literacy workshops and seminars offered by community

organizations, financial institutions, or educational institutions.

3. Financial News and Media: Stay informed about financial news and trends by reading reputable financial publications and watching financial news programs.

4. Practice and Application: Apply financial concepts in real life by creating budgets, setting up savings plans, and making investment decisions. Practical experience reinforces learning.

Goal Setting: Achieving Financial Success

Setting clear, achievable financial goals provides direction and motivation. Goals give purpose to financial decisions and help track progress.

Types of Financial Goals:

1. Short-Term Goals: Goals to be achieved within one year, such as building an emergency fund, paying off a small debt, or saving for a vacation.

2. Medium-Term Goals: Goals with a timeline of one to five years, such as saving for a down payment on a house, buying a car, or funding education.

3. Long-Term Goals: Goals that take more than five years to achieve, such as retirement savings, paying off a mortgage, or significant investment milestones.

SMART Goal Setting:

- Specific: Clearly define the goal. For example, "Save $5,000 for an emergency fund" is more specific than "Save money."

- Measurable: Ensure the goal can be tracked and measured. For example, "Save $500 per month for 10 months" provides a measurable target.

- Achievable: Set realistic goals that are attainable given your financial situation. Avoid setting goals that are too ambitious and likely to lead to frustration.

- Relevant: Align goals with your overall financial and life objectives. Ensure they are meaningful and relevant to your priorities.

- Time-Bound: Set a deadline for achieving the goal. For example, "Save $5,000 by December 31" creates a clear timeframe for completion.

Mindful Spending: Aligning Spending with Values

Mindful spending involves being intentional about how you spend money, ensuring that expenditures align with your values and financial goals. It encourages thoughtful decision-making and reduces unnecessary spending.

Strategies for Mindful Spending:

1. Reflect on Values: Identify your core values and financial priorities. Align spending with what truly matters to you, such as health, education, experiences, or savings.

2. Create a Spending Plan: Develop a spending plan that outlines how much money you will allocate to different categories, such as essentials, savings, and discretionary spending.

3. Track Spending: Monitor your spending regularly to ensure it aligns with your plan. Use budgeting apps or spreadsheets to keep track of expenses.

4. Limit Impulse Purchases: Implement a waiting period for non-essential purchases. For example, wait 24 hours before making a purchase to determine if it is necessary and aligns with your values.

5. Focus on Quality over Quantity: Prioritize spending on high-quality items that offer long-term value rather than accumulating cheap, low-quality goods.

6. Avoid Lifestyle Inflation: Resist the urge to increase spending as your income rises. Maintain a consistent lifestyle and allocate additional income to savings or investments.

Seeking Professional Advice: Getting Expert Help

Financial professionals can provide valuable guidance and expertise, helping you navigate complex financial decisions and achieve your goals.

Types of Financial Professionals:

1. Financial Advisors: Provide comprehensive financial planning and investment advice. They can help you

develop a financial plan, manage investments, and plan for retirement.

2. Credit Counselors: Offer advice on managing debt, improving credit scores, and developing budgets. They can also negotiate with creditors on your behalf.

3. Accountants and Tax Professionals: Assist with tax planning, preparation, and filing. They can help you maximize tax savings and ensure compliance with tax laws.

4. Estate Planners: Specialize in planning for the distribution of your assets after death. They can help you create wills, trusts, and other estate planning documents.

When to Seek Professional Advice:

1. Major Life Changes: Consult a financial professional during significant life events, such as marriage, divorce, buying a home, having children, or nearing retirement.

2. Complex Financial Situations: Seek expert help when dealing with complex financial situations, such as managing a large inheritance, business finances, or significant investments.

3. Debt Management: If you are struggling with debt, a credit counselor can provide strategies for repayment and improving financial health.

4. Tax Planning: Work with a tax professional to optimize your tax strategy, especially if you have complex tax situations, such as owning a business or multiple income streams.

Choosing a Financial Professional:

1. Credentials and Experience: Look for professionals with relevant credentials, such as Certified Financial Planner (CFP), Certified Public Accountant (CPA), or Accredited Financial Counselor (AFC). Ensure they have experience in the areas you need assistance with.

2. Fee Structure: Understand the fee structure of the financial professional. Some charge hourly rates, flat fees, or a percentage of assets under management. Choose a structure that aligns with your budget and needs.

3. Reputation and References: Research the professional's reputation and ask for references or testimonials from previous clients. Look for reviews and ratings online.

4. Personal Fit: Choose a financial professional you feel comfortable with and who understands your financial goals and values. A good rapport and trust are essential for a successful working relationship.

Additional Strategies for Enhancing Financial Well-Being

1. Emergency Fund: Build an emergency fund to cover unexpected expenses. Aim for three to six months' worth of living expenses in a readily accessible account.

2. Debt Reduction: Prioritize paying off high-interest debt to reduce financial stress and free up funds for savings and investments. Consider strategies like the debt snowball or debt avalanche method.

3. Retirement Planning: Start saving for retirement as early as possible. Contribute to retirement accounts such as 401(k)s, IRAs, or other pension plans. Take advantage of employer matching contributions if available.

4. Insurance Coverage: Ensure you have adequate insurance coverage for health, life, disability, and property. Insurance provides financial protection and peace of mind.

5. Regular Financial Reviews: Conduct regular reviews of your financial situation and goals. Adjust your plan as needed to stay on track and adapt to changes in your life or financial circumstances.

6. Financial Education: Continuously educate yourself about personal finance and stay informed about financial trends and changes in laws and regulations. Knowledge empowers you to make better financial decisions.

Enhancing financial well-being requires a combination of financial literacy, goal setting, mindful spending, and seeking professional advice when necessary. By implementing these strategies, individuals can take control of their finances, reduce stress, and achieve greater happiness and overall well-being. Building a solid financial foundation and making informed decisions contribute to a more secure and fulfilling life.

CHAPTER 16

THE FUTURE OF MONEY AND HAPPINESS

As technology and society continue to evolve, the relationship between money and happiness is also poised for significant changes. Emerging trends such as automation, universal basic income (UBI), and shifting work environments will play crucial roles in shaping future economic landscapes and individual well-being. This chapter explores these trends and their potential impact on the money-happiness nexus, speculating on both opportunities and challenges that lie ahead.

The Impact of Automation

Automation, driven by advances in artificial intelligence (AI) and robotics, is transforming industries and labor markets. While automation has the potential to enhance productivity and economic growth, it also raises important questions about employment, income distribution, and happiness.

Opportunities:

1. Increased Productivity: Automation can lead to significant productivity gains, reducing costs and potentially

lowering prices for consumers. This can enhance overall economic efficiency and living standards.

2. Reduced Repetitive Tasks: Automating repetitive and mundane tasks can free up human workers to focus on more creative, strategic, and fulfilling activities. This shift can improve job satisfaction and well-being.

3. New Job Creation: While some jobs may be displaced by automation, new jobs will emerge in fields such as AI development, robotics maintenance, and advanced data analysis. These roles may offer higher wages and better working conditions.

Challenges:

1. Job Displacement: Automation is expected to displace certain types of jobs, particularly those involving routine and manual tasks. Workers in these roles may face unemployment or the need to retrain for new careers.

2. Income Inequality: The benefits of automation may not be evenly distributed, potentially exacerbating income inequality. Workers with skills relevant to automated industries may prosper, while others may struggle to adapt.

3. Psychological Impact: The threat of job displacement and economic uncertainty can cause stress and anxiety, negatively affecting mental health and happiness.

Strategies for Adapting to Automation:

1. Lifelong Learning: Encourage and invest in lifelong learning and continuous education to help workers adapt to changing job markets and acquire new skills.

2. Social Safety Nets: Strengthen social safety nets, including unemployment benefits and retraining programs, to support workers affected by automation.

3. Policy Interventions: Implement policies that promote equitable distribution of the economic benefits of automation, such as progressive taxation and income support programs.

Universal Basic Income (UBI)

Universal Basic Income (UBI) is a policy proposal that involves providing all citizens with a regular, unconditional cash payment to ensure a basic standard of living. UBI is gaining attention as a potential solution to address income inequality and economic insecurity.

Opportunities:

1. Financial Security: UBI can provide a safety net for individuals, reducing financial stress and poverty. This financial security can enhance overall well-being and happiness.

2. Encouraging Innovation: With a guaranteed income, individuals may be more willing to pursue

entrepreneurial ventures, creative projects, or further education, fostering innovation and personal fulfillment.

3. Simplifying Welfare Systems: UBI can simplify existing welfare systems by replacing complex and often stigmatizing means-tested benefits with a straightforward, universal payment.

Challenges:

1. Cost and Funding: Implementing UBI on a national scale requires substantial financial resources. Determining how to fund UBI sustainably is a significant challenge.

2. Work Incentives: Critics argue that UBI might reduce the incentive to work, potentially leading to a decline in labor force participation. Addressing this concern is crucial for UBI's success.

3. Inflationary Pressure: There is a concern that UBI could lead to inflation if not carefully managed, as increased purchasing power might drive up prices for goods and services.

Strategies for Implementing UBI:

1. Pilot Programs: Conduct pilot programs to test UBI's feasibility, effectiveness, and impact on work incentives and economic behavior. Use the findings to inform policy decisions.

2. Gradual Implementation: Consider phased or regional implementation of UBI to manage costs and assess its impact incrementally.

3. Complementary Policies: Combine UBI with other policies, such as affordable housing and healthcare, to address broader economic and social challenges.

Changing Work Environments

The nature of work is evolving, influenced by factors such as remote work, the gig economy, and technological advancements. These changes have significant implications for work-life balance, job satisfaction, and happiness.

Opportunities:

1. Flexible Work Arrangements: Remote work and flexible schedules offer greater autonomy and work-life balance, allowing individuals to tailor their work environment to their personal needs and preferences.

2. Access to Global Talent: Advances in communication technology enable companies to tap into a global talent pool, fostering diversity and innovation.

3. Gig Economy Opportunities: The gig economy provides opportunities for freelance and contract work, allowing individuals to pursue varied and flexible career paths.

Challenges:

1. Job Security: Gig economy workers and remote employees may face job insecurity, lack of benefits, and irregular income, impacting financial stability and well-being.

2. Work-Life Boundaries: Remote work can blur the boundaries between work and personal life, leading to overwork and burnout if not managed effectively.

3. Isolation and Collaboration: Remote work can lead to social isolation and challenges in team collaboration, affecting job satisfaction and mental health.

Strategies for Adapting to Changing Work Environments:

1. Promote Work-Life Balance: Encourage policies and practices that promote work-life balance, such as flexible hours, paid time off, and mental ealth support.

2. Ensure Job Security and Benefits: Advocate for policies that provide gig workers and remote employees with access to benefits such as health insurance, retirement plans, and job protection.

3. Foster Social Connections: Implement initiatives to foster social connections and collaboration among remote workers, such as virtual team-building activities and regular check-ins.

The Role of Technology in Financial Management

Technology is revolutionizing financial management, providing tools and resources that can enhance financial well-being and happiness.

Opportunities:

1. Personal Finance Apps: Financial apps and platforms offer budgeting, saving, and investing tools that help individuals manage their finances more effectively and make informed decisions.

2. Automated Savings and Investing: Automated systems can simplify saving and investing by setting up recurring transfers and investment plans, making it easier to build wealth.

3. Access to Information: The internet provides access to a wealth of financial information and educational resources, empowering individuals to improve their financial literacy and decision-making.

Challenges:

1. Data Security and Privacy: The increased use of digital financial tools raises concerns about data security and privacy. Protecting personal information is crucial.

2. Over-Reliance on Technology: Dependence on technology for financial management can lead to complacency and a lack of understanding of fundamental financial principles.

3. Digital Divide: Not everyone has equal access to technology and the internet, creating disparities in financial management capabilities.

Strategies for Leveraging Technology:

1. Enhance Financial Literacy: Use technology to access educational resources and improve financial literacy. Participate in online courses, webinars, and financial planning tools.

2. Utilize Automation: Take advantage of automated saving and investing features to streamline financial management and ensure consistent progress toward financial goals.

3. Prioritize Security: Use secure platforms and regularly update passwords and security settings to protect personal financial information.

The future of money and happiness will be shaped by technological advancements, evolving work environments, and innovative economic policies. While these changes present significant opportunities for enhancing financial well-being and overall happiness, they also pose challenges that require thoughtful adaptation and proactive strategies. By embracing lifelong learning, promoting work-life balance, advocating for equitable policies, and leveraging technology responsibly, individuals and societies can navigate the complexities of the future and build a more prosperous and fulfilling world.

CHAPTER 17

CONCLUSION

The journey through this book has taken us on an exploration of the intricate relationship between money and happiness. We have delved into various aspects of financial well-being, psychological theories, cultural influences, and practical strategies to enhance happiness through effective financial management. This concluding chapter summarizes the key points discussed and offers final reflections on how individuals can navigate the complex interplay between money and happiness to lead fulfilling lives.

Key Insights from the Book

1. The Multifaceted Nature of Happiness:

- Happiness is a complex and multifaceted concept that encompasses psychological well-being, life satisfaction, and emotional fulfillment. Understanding these dimensions helps us appreciate that money is just one of many factors influencing happiness.

2. Historical and Cultural Perspectives:

- Different cultures and historical periods have varied perspectives on wealth and happiness. These cultural influences shape our attitudes toward money and highlight the importance of balancing material and non-material values.

3. Psychological Theories on Money and Happiness:

- Theories such as Maslow's Hierarchy of Needs, the Easterlin Paradox, and hedonic adaptation provide valuable insights into how financial resources impact well-being. They emphasize that beyond meeting basic needs, additional income has diminishing returns on happiness.

4. Financial Security and Basic Needs:

- Financial security is crucial for meeting basic needs and providing a stable foundation for happiness. Effective financial management helps reduce stress and create a sense of control over one's life.

5. Materialism and Its Discontents:

- Excessive focus on material possessions can lead to decreased happiness. Shifting the focus from possessions to experiences and relationships fosters long-term well-being and fulfillment.

6. The Psychological Benefits of Generosity and Altruism:

- Acts of generosity and altruism significantly boost happiness by creating a sense of purpose and strengthening social connections. Helping others enriches our lives and contributes to a more compassionate society.

7. The Role of Relationships and Social Connections:

- Strong relationships and social connections are fundamental to happiness. Money can influence relationships positively by providing stability and enabling shared experiences, but it can also create stress and conflict if not managed wisely.

8. Cultural and Societal Influences:

- Societal norms and cultural values play a significant role in shaping the relationship between money and happiness. Understanding these influences helps us navigate the expectations and pressures we face in our financial and personal lives.

9. Financial Management and Happiness:

- Effective financial management, including budgeting, saving, investing, and planning for the future, is essential for enhancing financial well-being. These practices reduce stress, provide security, and help achieve financial goals.

10. The Future of Money and Happiness:

- As technology and society evolve, the relationship between money and happiness will continue to change. Emerging trends such as automation, universal basic income, and shifting work environments present both opportunities and challenges for future well-being.

Final Reflections on Navigating Money and Happiness

The relationship between money and happiness is dynamic and influenced by various factors, including individual values, cultural norms, and societal changes. While financial resources are essential for meeting basic needs and providing security, true happiness extends beyond material wealth. Here are some final reflections on how individuals can navigate this complex interplay to lead fulfilling lives:

1. Align Financial Goals with Personal Values:

- Reflect on your core values and priorities. Align your financial goals and spending habits with what truly matters to you. This alignment ensures that your financial decisions contribute to your overall well-being and fulfillment.

2. Focus on Experiences and Relationships:

- Invest in experiences and relationships rather than accumulating material possessions. Shared experiences and strong social connections provide lasting happiness and enrich your life.

3. Practice Mindful Spending and Saving:

- Be intentional about how you spend and save money. Mindful financial management helps you make informed decisions, avoid unnecessary debt, and build a secure financial future.

4. Embrace Generosity and Altruism:

- Incorporate acts of generosity and altruism into your life. Helping others not only benefits them but also enhances your own sense of purpose and happiness.

5. Adapt to Changing Environments:

- Stay flexible and open to change. As technology and societal norms evolve, be prepared to adapt your financial strategies and goals to new realities.

6. Seek Balance and Well-Being:

- Strive for balance in all aspects of life. Ensure that your pursuit of financial success does not come at the expense of your health, relationships, and overall well-being.

7. Continual Learning and Growth:

- Commit to lifelong learning and personal growth. Continuously educate yourself about financial management, personal development, and the evolving relationship between money and happiness.

Concluding Thoughts

The quest for happiness is a fundamental human endeavor, and money, while important, is just one piece of the puzzle. By understanding the multifaceted nature of happiness and adopting effective financial strategies, individuals can navigate the complex interplay between wealth and well-being. The insights and lessons from this book provide a roadmap for achieving financial security and personal fulfillment, enabling you to lead a more balanced, content, and meaningful life.

As you continue your journey, remember that true happiness comes from a combination of financial stability, strong relationships, meaningful experiences, and a sense of purpose. Embrace these elements, and you will find that the pursuit of happiness is not just about accumulating wealth, but about creating a life that is rich in every sense.

Thank you for joining me on this exploration of money and happiness. May the knowledge and strategies shared in this book guide you toward a fulfilling and joyful life, where financial well-being and personal happiness go hand in hand.

APPENDICES

Appendix A: Financial Management Resources

Books:

1. "The Total Money Makeover" by Dave Ramsey: A practical guide to financial fitness, covering budgeting, saving, debt reduction, and wealth building.

2. "Your Money or Your Life" by Vicki Robin and Joe Dominguez: A comprehensive program for transforming your relationship with money and achieving financial independence.

3. "Rich Dad Poor Dad" by Robert T. Kiyosaki: Lessons on financial literacy, investing, and building wealth from the perspective of two contrasting father figures.

4. "The Millionaire Next Door" by Thomas J. Stanley and William D. Danko: Insights into the habits and characteristics of America's wealthiest individuals.

Online Courses:

1. Coursera: Offers various courses on personal finance, investing, and financial planning from top universities.

2. Udemy: Provides a wide range of courses on budgeting, debt management, and wealth-building strategies.

3. Khan Academy: Free courses on personal finance, including budgeting, saving, investing, and understanding credit.

Websites:

1. Investopedia: Comprehensive resource for investing education, financial terms, and market analysis.

2. NerdWallet: Personal finance website offering tools and advice on budgeting, credit cards, loans, and insurance.

3. The Balance: Provides practical advice on personal finance, including saving, investing, retirement planning, and tax strategies.

Financial Planning Tools:

1. Mint: A free budgeting app that tracks income, expenses, and savings goals.

2. YNAB (You Need A Budget): Budgeting software that helps users manage their money and save for future goals.

3. Personal Capital: A financial planning tool that offers investment tracking, retirement planning, and budgeting features.

Appendix B: Financial Goal Setting Templates

Short-Term Financial Goal Template:

Goal Description	Target Amount	Current Savings	Monthly Contribution	Target Date	Progress Notes
Emergency Fund	$5,000	$1,000	$400	12 months	
Vacation Fund	$2,000	$500	$150	10 months	

Medium-Term Financial Goal Template:

Goal Description	Target Amount	Current Savings	Monthly Contribution	Target Date	Progress Notes
Home Down Payment	$30,000	$10,000	$500	5 years	
Education Fund for Child	$15,000	$3,000	$250	3 years	

Long-Term Financial Goal Template:

Goal Description	Target Amount	Current Savings	Monthly Contribution	Target Date	Progress Notes
Retirement Savings	$500,000	$100,000	$1,000	20 years	
Investment Property	$100,000	$20,000	$400	15 years	

Appendix C: Sample Budget Template

Monthly Income:

Source	Amount
Salary	$3,500
Freelance	$500
Investment	$200
Total Income	$4,200

Monthly Expenses:

Category	Budgeted Amount	Actual Amount	Variance
Housing (Rent/Mortgage)	$1,200	$1,200	$0
Utilities	$200	$180	+$20
Groceries	$400	$450	-$50
Transportation	$300	$320	-$20
Insurance	$150	$150	$0
Savings/Investments	$500	$500	$0
Entertainment	$200	$250	-$50
Miscellaneous	$150	$100	+$50
Total Expenses	$3,100	$3,150	-$50

Savings Goals:

Goal Description	Target Amount	Current Savings	Monthly Contribution	Target Date	Progress Notes
Emergency Fund	$5,000	$2,000	$200	18 months	
Vacation Fund	$2,000	$500	$100	15 months	

Appendix D: Questions to Ask a Financial Advisor

1. Credentials and Experience:

- What are your professional qualifications and certifications?

- How many years of experience do you have in financial planning and advising?

2. Services Offered:

- What specific services do you provide (e.g., investment management, retirement planning, tax planning)?

- Can you provide a comprehensive financial plan tailored to my needs?

3. Fee Structure:

- How do you charge for your services (e.g., hourly rate, flat fee, percentage of assets under management)?

- Are there any additional costs or fees I should be aware of?

4. Investment Philosophy:

- What is your investment philosophy and approach to risk management?

- How do you select and monitor investments?

5. Client Communication:

- How often will we meet to review my financial plan and progress?

- How will you keep me informed about changes in my investments and financial situation?

6. References and Testimonials:

- Can you provide references or testimonials from current or past clients?

- Have you ever been subject to disciplinary action or complaints?

Appendix E: Mindful Spending Tips

1. Create a Spending Plan:

- List all your monthly income sources and expenses.

- Prioritize essential expenses and allocate funds for savings and discretionary spending.

2. Track Your Spending:

- Use budgeting apps or a spreadsheet to record and monitor your daily expenditures.

- Review your spending habits regularly to identify areas for improvement.

3. Avoid Impulse Purchases:
- Implement a waiting period (e.g., 24 hours) before making non-essential purchases.
- Reflect on whether the purchase aligns with your values and financial goals.

4. Focus on Quality Over Quantity:
- Invest in high-quality items that offer long-term value and satisfaction.
- Avoid accumulating low-quality, disposable goods that clutter your space and drain your finances.

5. Plan for Major Purchases:
- Save for major purchases in advance rather than relying on credit.
- Research and compare prices to ensure you get the best value for your money.

6. Limit Exposure to Advertising:

- Reduce exposure to advertising by unsubscribing from marketing emails and avoiding frequent visits to online shopping sites.

- Be mindful of the influence of social media and peer pressure on your spending decisions.

These appendices provide valuable resources, templates, and practical tips to help you manage your finances effectively and enhance your overall well-being. By incorporating these strategies into your financial planning, you can navigate the complex relationship between money and happiness with confidence and clarity.